MONSTERS
ZOMBIES
VAMPIRES
AND MORE!

This edition published by Parragon in 2012

Parragon
Queen Street House
4 Queen Street
Bath BA1 1HE, UK
www.parragon.com

Cover designed by Rachael Fisher
Cover illustrated by Nelson Evergreen

Published by arrangement with 3J Editores
Edificios Altos del Bosque, Calle 134 # 7–83, Torre 4, Piso 3, Oficina 432

Photos and images courtesy of 3J Editores.

Original publication:
Authors: Claudia Molina Rodríguez and Fernando Cortés Ramos
Editor: Claudia Molina Rodríguez, Degree in Psychology and Teaching, Masters in Education,
National Teacher Training University
Illustrators: Fernando Cortés Ramos, Andres Escobar, Francisco Garcia and Ivan Dario Espinel
Assistant illustrator: Francisco García García
Literary adaptations: Wilson Molina Rodríguez, graduate in Linguistics and Literature
Design: Alba Giraldo

ISBN 978-1-4454-8689-5

Printed in China

MONSTERS
ZOMBIES
VAMPIRES
AND MORE!

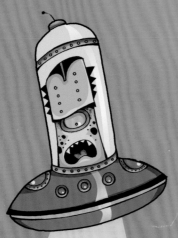

PaRragon

Bath · New York · Singapore · Hong Kong · Cologne · Delhi
Melbourne · Amsterdam · Johannesburg · Shenzhen

CONTENTS

INTRODUCTION

Prepare to be amazed and horrified by some of the most terrifying monsters ever created! Inside the pages of this book you'll find Frankenstein's Monster, Dracula, the werewolf, witches, King Kong, Bigfoot and a whole host of other scary beasts.

Read each terrible story (if you dare!), then find out about the facts behind the monsters. Find out who was the real-life inspiration for Count Dracula, discover what happened to people found guilty of witchcraft and read the shocking truth behind the tales of werewolves and vampires.

Don't forget to keep one eye looking over your shoulder as you read. You never know which of these ghastly creatures might be behind you....

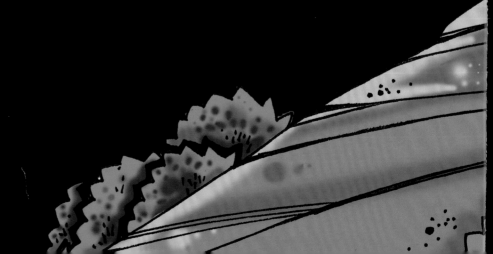

Frankenstein

Original story by Mary Shelley

Doctor Victor Frankenstein loved science and was keen to learn. He spent many hours, days and weeks locked in his laboratory, often trying out bold and dangerous experiments.

Doctor Frankenstein was desperate to discover the secret to life. One night, as he studied his books on the human body, he made a fantastic discovery. He found that electricity could bring a body to life! The doctor immediately decided to create his own living creature.

Frankenstein needed the perfect body parts for his creation. He crept out at night to morgues and cemeteries, quietly gathering parts from dead bodies. He took arms, legs, a heart, a liver and all the other parts he needed.

With the help of his assistant, Igor, Frankenstein carefully stitched the parts together. Finally, he screwed on the head using two large bolts. The result was a giant, ugly creature: Frankenstein's Monster.

Victor Frankenstein stood back and admired his creation. The Monster's skin was a pale, ghostly green, and his lips were deathly purple.

Thin metal wires connected the Monster to a machine that the doctor and Igor had built. They planned to use the machine to harness electricity from lightning. All they had to do was wait for a storm to strike.

Suddenly, a bolt of lightning lit up the sky and Doctor Frankenstein quickly flicked a switch on his machine. The Monster's body began to shudder. Seconds later, his eyes opened and he gave a long, deep sigh. The miracle was complete. Frankenstein's Monster was alive!

The Monster looked at Frankenstein and tried to speak, but his mouth would not form words. He was frustrated and confused. He stood up on his huge feet and stretched out his ugly hands. As he lurched forwards, Igor jumped in front of him with a torch. The Monster snatched the torch from Igor's hands and ran out into the night.

The Monster wandered around for many days. He ate fruit from the trees, drank water from the rivers and taught himself to hunt small animals. He gazed at the distant villages, too afraid to go near them.

One afternoon, he chased an animal and, without thinking, ran too close to a village. When the people who lived there saw the Monster, they fled screaming. The local hunter heard their cries and leapt up with his gun. Aiming quickly, the hunter fired.

The bullet hit the Monster in the side, and he yelled loudly. He ran back to the forest and cried alone. He vowed never to go near humans again.

Although he was hideous, the Monster was human at heart. He wanted to be normal, with friends and a home to live in. But he realized he was different, and this made him sad. He found a cave in the mountains and decided to live there alone.

After some time, the Monster came across an old, run-down shack near his hiding place. In it lived an old man and his grandchildren, who were very poor. The Monster watched every day as the children gathered food and firewood. At night, the family sat around their fire and the old man played his flute. The Monster was moved to tears by the music.

He decided to help the family in the hut. He hunted rabbits for them, picked fruit and collected firewood. The Monster left all of these gifts at the door of the family's hut and enjoyed seeing the happy, surprised looks on their faces.

Watching the family, the Monster learned about kindness and compassion. But he knew he would never sit with them or talk to them. This made him very sad and, finally, he decided to go to a place where there were no humans.

Rumour has it that the Monster still lives in a faraway place. He has no friends and sits alone in his humble cave. Sailors who travel near the South Pole say they have seen a giant man floating on giant blocks of ice.

What happened to his creator, Doctor Victor Frankenstein? It is said that he died alone and sad. We will never know what to believe, but one thing is sure: Frankenstein's Monster may still live among us!

The End

CREATING THE CREATURE

Mary Shelley

Mary Shelley

Frankenstein's Monster first came to life in the imagination of the author, Mary Shelley. Her novel was published in 1818.

Mary's mother died soon after Mary's birth, so Mary and her sister were raised by their father. In 1816, Mary married Percy Shelley and, when their first daughter died not long after her birth, Mary became extremely unhappy. Sadly, two more children died before Mary had Percy Florence, who survived.

In the last ten years of her life, Mary suffered from several diseases. At the age of 53, she died from a brain tumour.

One year after her death, Mary's family were cleaning out her beloved desk when they found Mary's personal notebook. They also found a single page wrapped around a silk parcel. It is thought to have contained some of her husband's ashes and the remains of his heart.

Percy Bysshe Shelley (1792–1822)

Percy Shelley was a writer and poet. Percy loved to visit William Godwin's book shop in London, where he met and fell in love with Mary when she was just 16 years old.

In 1814, Percy and Mary ran away to France. Six weeks later, feeling homesick and running out of money, they returned to England.

On 8 July, 1822, shortly before his 30th birthday, Percy was out sailing when his boat got caught in a storm. Percy Shelley drowned. His heart was removed before his cremation and was kept by Mary until she died.

Mary Shelley

Percy Bysshe Shelley

The Story Behind Frankenstein

The first edition of Frankenstein was published in London in 1818. Mary Shelley's name did not appear on the book until the second edition, published in 1823.

During the rainy summer of 1816, Mary and Percy visited a poet called Lord Byron in Switzerland. Due to bad weather, the group spent a lot of time indoors. They talked about the experiments of Erasmus Darwin (grandfather of Charles Darwin), who had apparently tried to bring dead things back to life.

The friends also discussed the recent discovery that electricity could make the muscles of a body move. Inspired by this, and by reading ghost stories, the trio decided to each write their own supernatural tale.

Not long after this, Mary had a dream that developed into the idea of Frankenstein's Monster. At first she began to write a short story, but Percy Shelley encouraged Mary to turn it into a full novel.

How does the Monster feel?

In Mary Shelley's original story, Frankenstein's Monster catches a glimpse of his reflection. This is his reaction: "How I was terrified when I viewed myself in a transparent pool! At first, I started back, unable to believe that it was indeed I who was reflected; and when I became fully convinced that I was in reality the monster that I am, I was filled with the bitterest sensations of despondence (sadness) and mortification (shame). Alas!"

The name 'Frankenstein' means 'stone of the Franks' in German. It is associated with Castle Frankenstein, which Mary Shelley might have heard of.

THE GRIPPING FACTS

What is Science Fiction?

Frankenstein is thought by many to be the very first science fiction novel. Science fiction describes things that do not really exist but explains them in a way that seems real. Stories may take place in the past, present, future or even in an alternative time. The characters featured in these stories might be humans, robots, androids, cyborgs or strange imaginary creatures.

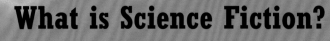

What messages does the story of *Frankenstein* give us about science and technology?

The Monster is confused, frustrated and sad throughout most of the story. His reaction to his creation is an example of the dangers of technology.

The story also shows how we all need love and acceptance from our parents and from society. The Monster desperately wants to fit in, but eventually realizes he will never be like everybody else.

H. G. Wells (1866–1946)

Wells was a writer, novelist, historian and philosopher. He made an important contribution to the world of science fiction and, in 1997, his name was added to the Science Fiction Hall of Fame.

TEN POPULAR SCIENCE FICTION STORIES:

- FRANKENSTEIN
- JOURNEY TO THE CENTRE OF THE EARTH
- 20,000 LEAGUES UNDER THE SEA
- THE ISLAND OF DOCTOR MOREAU
- THE TIME MACHINE
- WAR OF THE WORLDS
- THE INVISIBLE MAN
- NINETEEN EIGHTY-FOUR
- I, ROBOT
- DUNE

TEN OF THE MOST POPULAR SCIENCE FICTION MOVIES OF ALL TIME:

- AVATAR
- FRANKENSTEIN
- E.T.
- STAR WARS
- ALIEN
- THE MATRIX
- TERMINATOR
- WAR OF THE WORLDS
- BRAZIL
- I, ROBOT

Jules Verne (1828–1905)

Together with H. G. Wells, Jules Verne is considered one of the fathers of science fiction. Verne's stories cleverly predicted the invention of television, helicopters, submarines and spacecraft.

THE LABORATORY

Get the creeps

What do you need?
- A plastic comb
- Your hair

1. Rub the comb vigorously against your hair.

2. Slowly pull the comb away.

3. The all-powerful comb has made your hair stand on end. Creepy!

What happened?
Static electricity made your hair stand on end. Rubbing things together can produce an electrical charge. This makes some things move closer and others move away. In this case, your hairs became electrically charged and moved away from each other.

Make a compass

What do you need?

- A small bottle with a cap or lid
- A needle
- Thread
- A wooden stick
- A magnet

1 Ask an adult to make a hole in the centre of the bottle's lid. Put the lid back on the bottle.

2 Tie the thread around the middle of the needle.

3 Pass the needle and thread through the hole in the bottle's lid. The needle should be suspended inside the bottle. Now tie the other end of the thread to the stick.

4 Remove the needle from the bottle and carefully rub it against the magnet about 30 times in the same direction.

5 Put the needle back into the bottle and cover it with the lid. Slowly turn the bottle and you will find that the needle always points north. Frankenstein's Monster could have used this to find the South Pole!

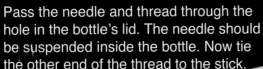

Keep magnets away from magnetic media, such as televisions, credit cards and cassette tapes.

The Loch Ness Monster

"Nessie," as this monster is commonly known, is a legendary creature, said to live in a lake called Loch Ness in Scotland. There is little scientific proof that Nessie exists, but people still claim to have seen her. Some have even taken photos of what they thought was the creature.

The first description of this monster appeared in a local newspaper in 1868. The article described an enormous and mysterious fish living in the depths of the loch.

In the 1930s, another newspaper published an article called "A Weird Experience at Loch Ness". It describes how two fishermen came across a gigantic creature, which they claimed almost destroyed their boat.

In 1933, a local couple were out walking around the lake. Suddenly, they saw what they thought was a humongous animal surface and dive back down into the water. Their story appeared in the newspapers. It caused such a sensation that reporters were sent to Scotland from hundreds of kilometres away to find out more about the monster.

Rewards were offered to anyone who could produce evidence that the monster existed, and a large sum of money was offered to anyone who captured it. A huge number of fortune-hunters came to Scotland to search for the famous monster. Many of them wanted to capture it, while others just wanted to catch a glimpse of it, so that they could tell the world.

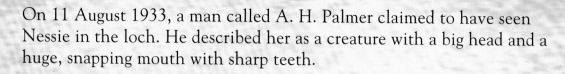

On 11 August 1933, a man called A. H. Palmer claimed to have seen Nessie in the loch. He described her as a creature with a big head and a huge, snapping mouth with sharp teeth.

The first photograph of the creature was taken by the surgeon R. K. Wilson on 19 April 1933. The picture seemed to show an enormous creature with a long neck, gliding through the water.

Many people believed this picture was evidence that the monster existed. Experts have examined the image, and some decided that it could be a plesiosaur, an animal that lived at the same time as dinosaurs.

Since the 1960s, Loch Ness has been thoroughly searched for more evidence of a monster. During the early 1970s, a group of investigators led by Robert Rines explored the depths of the lake, taking underwater pictures.

These images became famous because, once again, they seemed to show an animal that looked like a plesiosaur.

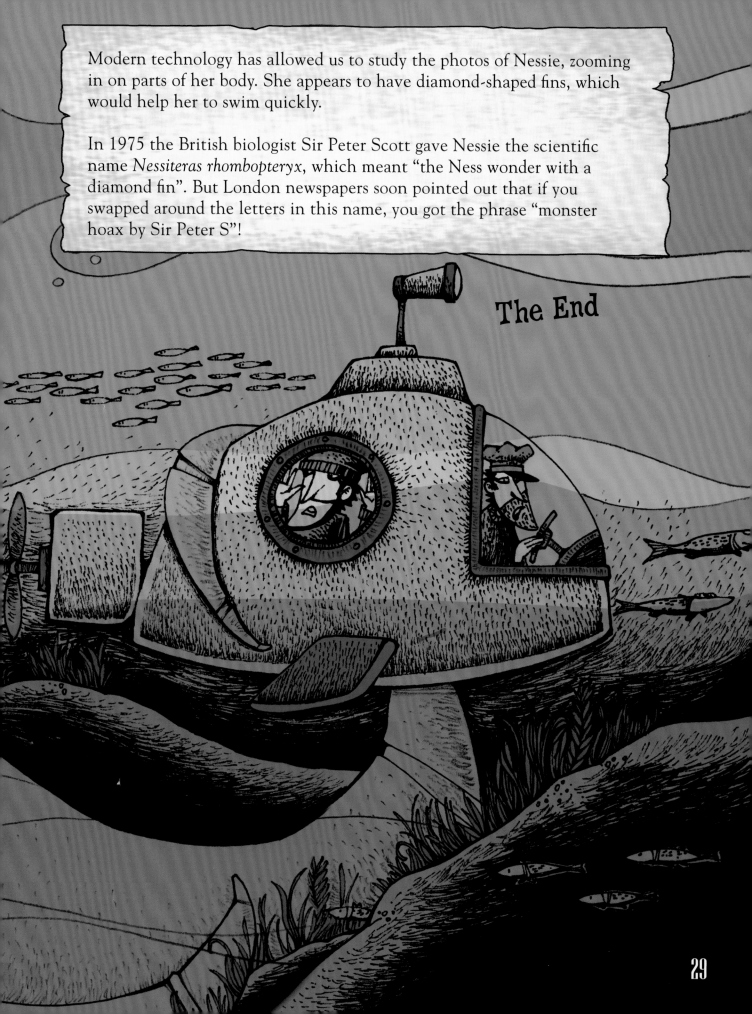

Modern technology has allowed us to study the photos of Nessie, zooming in on parts of her body. She appears to have diamond-shaped fins, which would help her to swim quickly.

In 1975 the British biologist Sir Peter Scott gave Nessie the scientific name *Nessiteras rhombopteryx*, which meant "the Ness wonder with a diamond fin". But London newspapers soon pointed out that if you swapped around the letters in this name, you got the phrase "monster hoax by Sir Peter S"!

The End

CREATING THE CREATURE

Robert Rines

Robert Rines was an American lawyer and member of the Loch Ness Phenomena Investigation Bureau. Rines led the expedition taking underwater photos of the Loch Ness Monster in 1972. His camera caught an image of a creature about 13.7 metres long and a neck 1.2-1.5 metres long. The film was sent to the United States of America and, after the images had been processed, a diamond-shaped fin was clearly visible.

Robert Rines

The naturalist Peter Scott, who was also a member of the Loch Ness Phenomena Investigation Bureau, said:

"Most people up to now have thought that we were lunatics for thinking there was something there. I am convinced that these photographs show the animals that gave rise to the legend of Loch Ness."

"The most important thing that you can see is the fin. No whales or dolphins have this type of fin. But there are fins with the same general form in the fossil records of prehistoric reptiles."

These findings allowed Nessie to be added to an official register of protected British species. Robert Rines dedicated the last 37 years of his life to the search for Nessie. He died on 1 November 2009.

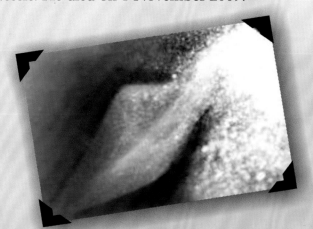

A photo of one of Nessie's diamond-shaped fins, taken by Robert Rines in 1972

The Origin of the Loch Ness Monster

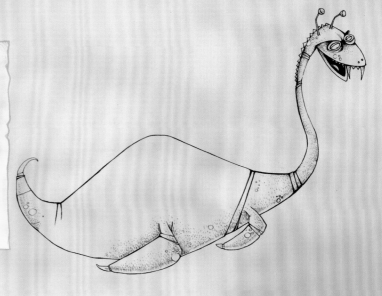

According to people's descriptions,
the Loch Ness Monster looks like a plesiosaur. This is an extinct prehistoric reptile from the Mesozoic Era, which lasted from around 250 million years ago to 65 million years ago. It was the time when dinosaurs roamed the land.

Most plesiosaurs were gigantic animals with large bodies adapted for life in the water. They had long, slim necks, small heads, fin-shaped legs and short tails.

However, there are reasons to doubt the theory that Nessie is a plesiosaur.

Plesiosaurs needed to come to the surface regularly to breathe. If Nessie were a plesiosaur, she would often be seen at the surface of the loch.

Many experts also think that such a large creature could not survive in a lake because it would not find enough food to eat.

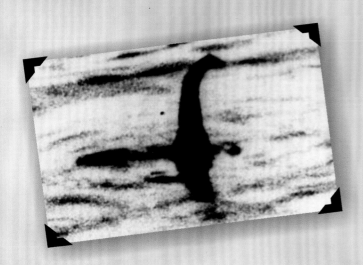

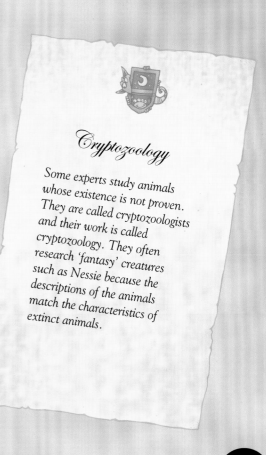

Cryptozoology

Some experts study animals whose existence is not proven. They are called cryptozoologists and their work is called cryptozoology. They often research 'fantasy' creatures such as Nessie because the descriptions of the animals match the characteristics of extinct animals.

STRANGE

BUT TRUE

Loch Ness is the largest body of fresh water in Britain. It is 36 kilometres long and 230 metres deep. That's as long as 750 Olympic-size swimming pools placed end to end and as deep as 10 on top of each other — plenty of room for a monster to hide in!

The first recorded sighting of Nessie was way back in the year 565, when St Columba stopped the beast attacking one of his followers, who had jumped into the water to catch a boat that was drifting away.

Wondering what the Loch Ness Monster might eat? Some people think zoo-plankton: other giant sea creatures eat these tiny organisms, so why not Nessie? Others say Nessie must eat fish — with an estimated 27 tonnes of fish in the Loch, there's certainly enough to go around!

If you're thinking that all the Nessie sightings must have happened a long time ago, think again! The most recent one was in March 2011, when local resident Jan Hargreaves and her husband Simon caught a glimpse of a long, black neck poking out of the water....

THE HIDDEN FACTS

Extinct or alive?

It's time to discover some other very mysterious creatures....

Morgan Esfinge Butterfly
In 1862, Charles Darwin suggested that there must have once been an insect that was capable of reaching the pollen at the bottom of the orchid flower.
In 1903, a white butterfly was discovered that could do exactly that!

Giant Squid
This fascinating creature measures 15–20 metres in length and can weigh up to one tonne. Its enormous tentacles make up most of its body. The giant squid belongs to the cephalopod family, which also includes octopuses and cuttlefish. Giant squid have been found in deep oceans around New Zealand.

Okapi
The okapi is closely related to the giraffe. Okapi are known as 'living fossils' because they are very similar to animals found in fossils dating from around 50 million years ago. Like giraffes, okapi have short bodies, long legs, wide ears and short horns. Their legs are white with black stripes, like a zebra.

The okapi lives in the jungles of Congo and Uganda. This beautiful species is now endangered, which means that it is rare and could become extinct.

Coelacanth
Coelacanths are large fish that first appeared on Earth nearly 400 million years ago. The fish are blue-grey in colour and have distinctive lobe-fins. They can grow to over 1.25 metres long and may weigh more than 65 kilograms. They live at depths of between 150 and 200 metres.

For many years, coelacanths were believed to be extinct. But, in 1938, a live coelacanth was caught. A second specimen was found in 1952 in the Comoros Islands in the Indian Ocean, and another in 1998 in Indonesia. The rare fish is now a protected species.

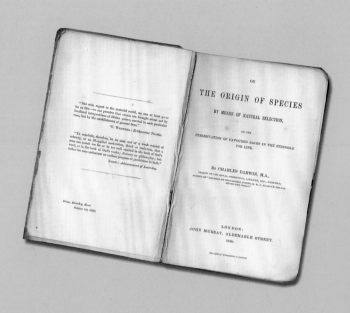

Charles Darwin
(1809–1882)

Charles Darwin was a scientist who loved finding out about mysterious creatures and nature. As a child, he enjoyed exploring gardens, collecting beetles and anything else he found to be interesting.

Darwin went to medical school but left because he disliked performing surgery. Later on, he studied geology and took part in an expedition to explore the coast of South America. On this five-year voyage, Darwin became even more excited about science and nature.

Darwin went on to write a famous book called *On the Origin of Species*. It introduced the idea that species evolved over time, with the fittest animals surviving to pass on their characteristics. Darwin's book also suggested that humans had evolved from apes. Not everyone was happy about this!

THE LABORATORY

Scientists, get ready! Can foil float?

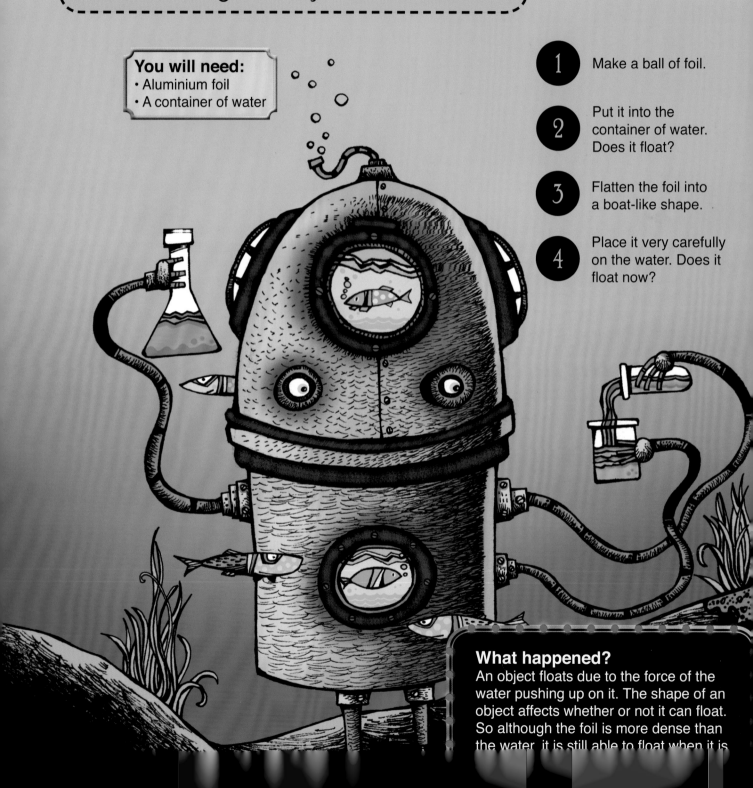

You will need:
• Aluminium foil
• A container of water

1 Make a ball of foil.

2 Put it into the container of water. Does it float?

3 Flatten the foil into a boat-like shape.

4 Place it very carefully on the water. Does it float now?

What happened?
An object floats due to the force of the water pushing up on it. The shape of an object affects whether or not it can float. So although the foil is more dense than the water, it is still able to float when it is

Do you float better in the sea or in a pool?

You will need:
- One egg
- One glass
- Water and salt

1 Fill the glass with water until it is one-third full.

2 Add salt to the water until it stops dissolving. There should be no salt at the bottom of the glass.

3 Gently place the egg in the glass. See how it floats on the salt water.

4 Slowly pour some more water into the glass, until it is full. Notice what happens to the egg.

What happened?
The egg floats in the middle of the glass between the fresh water and the salt water, which have not yet mixed. This is because salt water is more dense than the egg and pushes it towards the fresh water. You can float better in the sea than in a swimming pool because salt water is more dense than fresh water and pushes you up with a greater force.

Dracula

Original story by Bram Stoker

My name is Professor Abraham van Helsing, and I have a terrifying story to tell....

My tale begins with a young lawyer called Jonathan Harker, and a journey he made to Transylvania. Jonathan needed to see the mysterious Count Dracula about buying some buildings in London.

As soon as he entered the Count's castle, Jonathan shuddered with fear. The Count was a strange-looking man. He was also extremely curious about Jonathan's life in London, especially his fiancée, the beautiful Mina Murray....

Before long, Jonathan began to notice many strange things. The Count hid away during the day, only appearing at night. He never ate or drank, and his shadow always seemed to have a life of its own. Stranger still, the Count had no reflection in the mirror.

One day, Jonathan found he was unable to leave the castle. He had been taken prisoner! As he planned his escape, he was visited by three terrifying vampires – the brides of Dracula – who drank Jonathan's blood until he was very weak.

Meanwhile, Count Dracula had a plan. He got ready to travel to England.

Back in London, Mina was worried about Jonathan. She waited anxiously for him with her friend, Lucy.

One stormy day, a boat arrived on the English coast, bringing Count Dracula. He had travelled from Transylvania in a coffin, climbing out at night to feed on the crew. By the time the boat reached England, all of the sailors were dead!

As the days passed, Lucy began to look sick. She became pale and weak, and two strange holes appeared in her neck. At first, her friends thought it was some kind of disease, but when her health did not improve, they asked me for medical advice. I gave her blood transfusions, but these did not save her. Soon, poor Lucy died.

Shortly after Lucy's death, stories appeared about a beautiful woman who was biting local children. I immediately guessed what had happened. Lucy had been attacked by a vampire – an 'undead' creature that feeds on human blood so that it can live forever. Then poor Lucy had become a vampire herself and had risen from her grave to feed!

One night, I visited Lucy's grave with a group of her friends. It was empty! We searched for the creature she had become and, when we finally found it, drove a stake through its heart. The creature would feed no more, and our friend Lucy could now rest in peace.

After this, we received some good news. Jonathan had escaped from Dracula's castle! He returned to London and explained what had happened to him. We decided that Count Dracula must be the vampire that had attacked Lucy! Along with Lucy's friends, I vowed to find the Count and stop him from hurting anyone else.

Jonathan had the addresses of the Count's buildings in London. Together, we visited each one in turn, hoping to find him. Instead, we found that the Count had turned many more people into vampires. Eventually, we managed to kill them all.

When we finally found Count Dracula, he bit Mina! Armed with stakes and crosses, we attacked the Count. Just as we were about to kill him, he changed into a flurry of creepy bats. They flapped away into the darkness, back to Transylvania.

Realizing we must follow the bats, the group of us planned a vampire-hunting expedition and packed our bags. After a long journey, we reached the Count's castle.

When the castle door opened, we were faced with three horrifying figures that Jonathan had met before – the brides of Dracula! Fearing for our lives, we rounded up the three vampires and struck stakes through their hearts. Their bodies immediately crumbled to the ground.

Having defeated the brides, we crept into the depths of the castle. Suddenly, there was a bone-chilling howl. No one but Dracula could make that terrible sound! He had sensed the death of his brides, and he was angry.

In his grief, Dracula stormed out to attack us, but he made a terrible mistake. As he moved from the shadows, he stepped into the sunlight – a vampire's worst enemy. While he was dazzled by the light, we plunged a stake through his heart. The mighty Dracula fell apart before our very eyes.

It has now been over two years since these events. You will be relieved to hear that Mina survived the vampire's bite and made a full recovery. Mina and Jonathan got married, at last, and they now have a healthy young child. Together, the three of them live a full and happy life.

The End

STRANGE BUT TRUE

The story of Dracula first appeared in Bram Stoker's novel in 1897. Since then, the Vampire Count has made more appearances in TV shows and movies than any other fictional character, except for Sherlock Holmes!

Believe it or not, Count Dracula's dramatic gestures were based on a real person — the famous actor Henry Irving, who was manager at a theatre where Bram Stoker worked for 20 years.

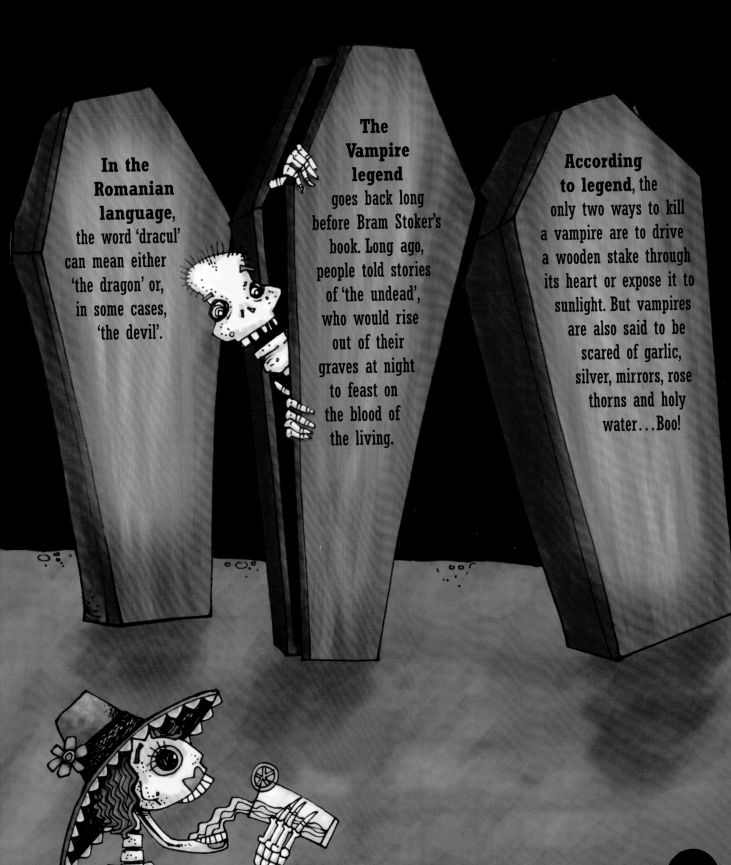

In the Romanian language, the word 'dracul' can mean either 'the dragon' or, in some cases, 'the devil'.

The Vampire legend goes back long before Bram Stoker's book. Long ago, people told stories of 'the undead', who would rise out of their graves at night to feast on the blood of the living.

According to legend, the only two ways to kill a vampire are to drive a wooden stake through its heart or expose it to sunlight. But vampires are also said to be scared of garlic, silver, mirrors, rose thorns and holy water…Boo!

THE GRUESOME FACTS

Blood

Blood is a liquid that flows through our capillaries, veins and arteries. It is made of red blood cells, white blood cells and plasma. Its red colour comes from a protein called haemoglobin, which is found in red blood cells. The amount of blood a person has in their body depends on their age, weight and sex.

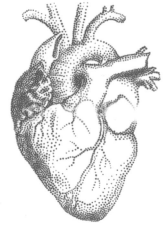

Blood circulation

The circulatory system is powered by the heart (above), which acts as a pump. Blood is carried away from the heart to all parts of the body by tube-like arteries. Here, it passes into tiny capillaries, which carry the blood to the body's cells. The blood returns to the heart through veins.

Blood types

The Austrian Karl Landsteiner (below) discovered that people have different blood types. He also discovered that you can only transfer blood from one person to another if they have the same blood type. This is called a transfusion. There are four blood types: A, B, AB and O. We inherit our blood type from our parents.

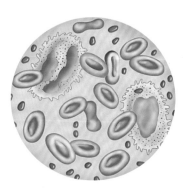

First blood transfusion
The first human blood transfusion was given to mathematician Jean Baptiste Denis in June 1667.

Blood donation

People can volunteer to donate blood to be used in hospitals for operations. In some countries, 'blood banks' help to gather and store this blood until it is used.

Bloodsucking animals

Vinchuca bug
This small insect is about the size of an eraser and is found in South America. It likes to hide in hay, but emerges at night to suck human blood.

Mosquito
Female mosquitoes suck blood, which they need to produce eggs. Mosquitoes are known to spread diseases, such as malaria and yellow fever.

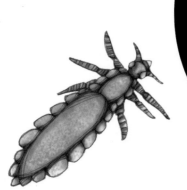

Vampire bat
This tiny bat measures just 7.5–10 centimetres wide. It feeds on the blood of mammals and birds, using its sensors to identify the most blood-filled areas of the body, and biting its victim with its fangs. Although it sucks very little blood, the vampire bat carries deadly diseases, such as rabies.

Leeches
Leeches are a type of worm. They sniff out their victims before biting, using a special chemical on their tongues to remain stuck to their victim. With three jaws and about 300 teeth, leeches can suck as much blood as they need. They are sometimes used by doctors to suck patients' blood and clean dirty wounds.

Lice
These tiny parasites live in human hair. They feed on small amounts of blood that they draw from the scalp, and attach their eggs to the hair of their victims.

Fleas
Fleas are tiny insects that feed on the blood of mammals. They use their powerful hind legs to spring from one animal to the next.

Ticks
Ticks are blood-sucking arachnids. When they find their victims, they use their skin-piercing mouths to suck blood. They can go several months without feeding.

THE LABORATORY

Make an origami bat

1 Fold your piece of paper in half diagonally and open it out. You will need this crease later on.

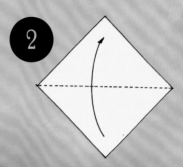

2 Now fold the paper in half diagonally the other way to make a triangle. Your triangle should be pointing upwards.

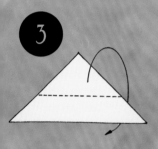

3 Fold both flaps of the triangle towards the back. Look at the line in this picture to help you make your fold.

4 Place your paper flat on the table. Fold each side inwards about a centimetre, towards the crease you made earlier. Use the picture to guide you.

5 You have just folded the wings and your bat should look like this. Now turn it over.

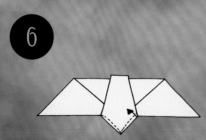

6 Make two folds to shape the bat's tail. The folds should be in the same place as the dotted lines in this picture.

7 Finally, fold down the flat end of the middle section to make the bat's head. Turn it over and your bat is finished!

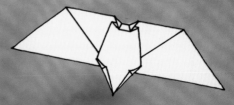

WITCHES

Real or make-believe...?

Hundreds of years ago, most people believed that witches were real. Anyone who was thought to be a witch was badly punished – even if they had done nothing wrong! Today, most people think that witches are only make-believe. But just imagine if they were real....

If witches were real, they would be very clever. They would probably spend a lot of time studying, experimenting and creating new spells and potions, which could be used for good or bad.

Their spells might make animals talk, or turn people into beasts. Other spells might keep away unwanted visitors, or protect people and villages from harm.

Nobody is born with magical powers, so witches would have to work hard to get their spells and powers just right. Practice makes perfect!

spells and potions. But anyone who bought a potion from a witch would have to watch out.... She might put them under her spell instead!

Trainee witches would probably start learning at a very young age. They would go to witch school, where they would learn spells and magic from a teacher. They would need to have a very good memory to remember everything!

Some say that witches would get together on nights when there is a full moon, and also on 31 October – Halloween. They would climb onto their broomsticks, zoom across the night sky, then gather together to swap spells and potions.

Some people think that witches would not be very friendly. Instead of living with other people, witches would prefer to live on their own, or spend time out in the wild, with just a cat to keep them company.

Witches like these probably aren't real at all. There is certainly no proof that they exist. It's just as well – it means you're safe from falling under any nasty spells!

The End

CREATING THE CREATURE

The History of the Witch

In ancient Greece and Rome, people believed that witches were real and could fly, turn themselves into animals and cast spells. They told stories about Circe, a goddess of magic who used special potions.

Circe

In the Old Testament – a part of the Bible – no one was allowed to practise witchcraft. Anyone thought to be a witch was put to death. The Old Testament also said that witches could bring the dead back to life.

The Old Testament

Many people thought that witches were God's enemy. In 1184, the Christian Church decided to put an end to witchcraft. Over the next few hundred years, large numbers of people were accused of being witches, including a great Italian scientist, Galileo Galilei.

The Witches of Salem

In 1692 and 1693, a number of famous witch trials took place in Salem, a town in Massachusetts. At these trials, the accused witches were asked questions in a courtroom. Then a judge decided whether or not they were guilty of witchcraft. People living in Salem were very religious. Most of them were afraid of witches.

Altogether, more than 150 people were arrested for making contact with the spirit world. Nineteen men and women were put to death. No proof was ever found to show that they were guilty.

Today, the town of Salem is a tourist attraction, and thousands of visitors go there every year to see where the witch trials took place.

Hunting Witches

Witch hunts spread across Europe between 1400 and 1700. People accused of being witches were forced to confess, even if it wasn't true! They were often tortured, locked in a tower or dungeon or sentenced to death. Many innocent people were killed.

Galileo was put on trial in 1633

During the trials, suspected witches had to do tests. One test was to walk on fire, because it was believed that a witch could walk on flames without feeling pain.

In another test, the person was tied up and thrown into deep water. If she floated, she was believed to be a witch, and was killed. If she sank, she was innocent, but she drowned. The accused person usually died during these tests, since they weren't actually a witch and didn't have any powers at all!

Suspects were also forced to name other witches they had met at witches' meetings. If found guilty, they were often burned at the stake. Although most victims of witch hunts were women, some men were found guilty of witchcraft too.

Arthur Miller

Arthur Miller was born on 17 October 1915, in the city of New York. He studied journalism at the University of Michigan and won several major awards, including the Pulitzer Prize.

Arthur Miller

He wrote a play called *The Crucible*, based on the Salem witch trials. The play was first performed on Broadway in 1953, and was made into a movie in 1996. Miller died in 2005.

STRANGE

BUT TRUE

A group of witches is known
as a 'coven', meaning 'a gathering'
in medieval Scottish. Spookily, covens
were thought to have 13 members —
an unlucky number for some!

As well as mixing potions and casting spells, people thought witches could write special symbols on objects to give them special powers, curse a person by burning a wax doll replica of that person and use mirrors and other shiny objects to see into the future. Hocus pocus!

Black cats have often been seen as symbols of evil, because of their connection to witches. In Medieval Europe, large numbers of black cats were killed because people thought they were witches in disguise. Unbelievable!

THE SOARING FACTS

In case you haven't got a broomstick, here are some other ways to fly.

Flight

Throughout history, man has wanted to fly like a bird. Many legends exist about flying, from witches on broomsticks to the story of Icarus.

Icarus and his father, Daedalus, were prisoners who wanted to escape from an island. They built wings using feathers and wax, and flew away. But Icarus flew too close to the Sun. His wings began to melt and he fell into the ocean!

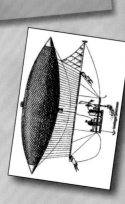

18th Century
Humans began to explore the world of aviation and flight, starting with the creation of hot-air balloons. The Montgolfier Brothers were two of the most successful inventors. They created several balloons used in many flights.

19th Century
- **1800**

George Cayley created a glider that was controlled by the tail. The pilot had to sit in the middle of the glider to balance it.

- **1852**

French engineer Henri Giffard invented an airship that was controlled by steering wheels and motors.

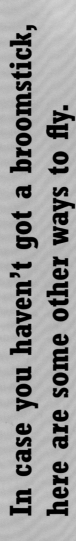

- **1874**
Felix du Temple built the first aluminium glider.

20th Century

- **1903**
The Wright Brothers made the first successful powered flight in a heavier-than-air plane.

- **1906**
Brazilian aviator Alberto Santos-Dumont made the first successful flight of an airplane in Europe.

- **1910**
The first commercial flight took place, carrying cargo to make a profit. It lasted 57 minutes, covering 105 kilometres.

- **1914**
Technology advanced enormously during World War I, and planes were built to carry weapons. These planes came in many shapes and sizes, and carried out important roles, such as spotting the enemy, dropping bombs and fighting enemy aircraft.

- **1918–39**
This was the Golden Age of Aviation, when huge changes took place. In 1927, Charles Lindbergh became the first person to fly by himself across the Atlantic Ocean, from America to Paris, without stopping.

- **1929**
Airship technology advanced, and a large airship made the first flight around the world. It was named a 'Zeppelin' after its German inventor, Ferdinand von Zeppelin.

- **1938**
The first flight of the Boeing 307 took place. This plane had a pressurized cabin, which meant it could fly much higher than earlier planes.

- **1939–45**
Airplanes were widely used throughout World War II.

- **1947**
Chuck Yeager became the first person to fly faster than the speed of sound in his Bell X-1 rocket-plane.

21st Century
Robot planes, which do not have a pilot, are used above battlefields to spy on enemy soldiers and fire missiles at enemy positions.

THE LABORATORY

The magic of air

What do you need?
- A cork
- A bucket of water
- A glass

1. Place the cork on the surface of the water in the bucket.

2. Turn the glass upside-down and place it over the cork. Push the glass down into the water.

3. Slowly turn the glass the right way up. Watch the cork.

What happened?

When the glass went underwater, the cork travelled with it and stayed at the base of the glass. As you turned the glass, bubbles came up toward the surface, the glass filled with water, and the cork travelled up. The glass was full of a clear substance that pushed the water and the cork, and then moved up through the water inside the bubbles. This clear substance was a gas called air.

THE FLY

ORIGINAL STORY BY GEORGE LANGELAAN

My name is Francois and I have a shocking story to tell. It begins one night, when I was sound asleep. I was suddenly awoken by the telephone ringing loudly. In a daze, I answered the phone.

My brother Andre's wife, Helene, replied in a strange voice. She told me that she had murdered Andre! She begged me to call the police, then meet her at a factory in town. I asked her to explain what had happened, but she hung up.

When I arrived at the factory with the police, we were met with a terrible scene. My brother's head and arm lay crushed in a large machine. They were completely destroyed.

The police spent the next few days looking into the murder, but found nothing to explain that night's events. Helene was sent to a special hospital for mentally ill people. I was asked to care for her son, Philippe.

We visited Helene often. She seemed to spend a lot of time killing flies, but I thought that was part of her madness.

One day, Philippe told me he had found a fly, and asked me if I knew how long it would live. I wondered why flies seemed so important to this family. Could flies have something to do with my brother's death?

I went to see Helene and told her that Philippe had found a fly. She immediately became nervous and told me we should kill it. After calming her down, I asked Helene what had happened. She passed me a piece of paper, saying it would explain everything. It was her confession.

Helene's confession explained how my brother, a famous scientist, had been working on something incredible. Andre had been doing experiments with teleportation – transporting something from one place to another in the blink of an eye.

He had made two teleportation machines. The first machine made an object disintegrate – fall apart – then sent it to the second machine, which put the object back together again.

I was amazed as I read Helene's story. Andre had successfully teleported simple objects from one machine to the other – teleportation worked!

Soon, Andre experimented with his first living creature – Helene's pet cat. Unfortunately, the experiment was not successful. The cat had been disintegrated, but Andre could not put it together again. Helene was very upset, but she forgave him.

Eventually, Andre succeeded in teleporting animals. He was thrilled at his discovery, and wanted to try to teleport himself. Helene begged him not to do it, but Andre was determined.

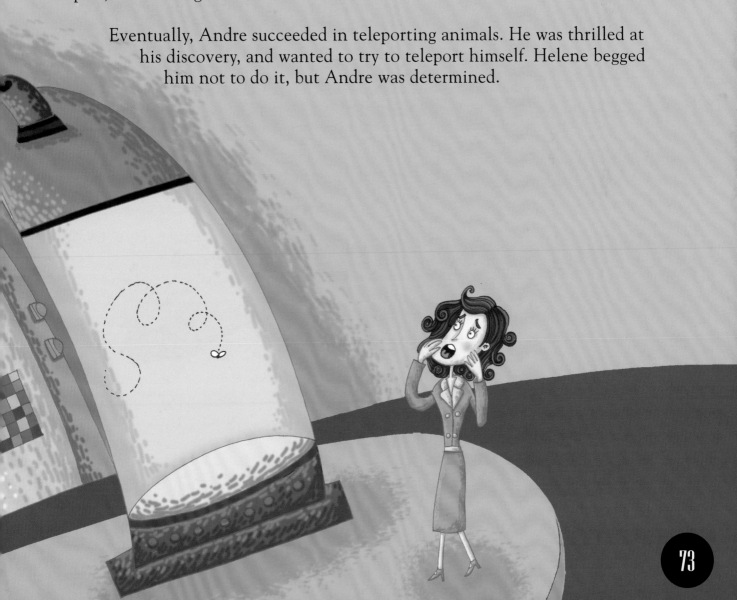

Andre turned on the first machine and lay on it, waiting. Soon, he disintegrated and appeared in the second machine. The experiment seemed to have worked, but afterwards Andre found that his head and arms had changed. He looked like a giant fly!

A fly must have buzzed into the machine with Andre, and when his body had been put back together, he had become part-fly, part-human.

Helene was terrified. Andre told her that the only way to fix him was to find the same fly that had flown into the machine.

Shortly after the experiment, Philippe had caught a very strange-looking fly with a white head and arms. Helene had told Philippe to set the fly free! She felt horrible. She hunted for the fly, but could not find it.

Meanwhile, Andre became more and more like a fly. He began to make a strange buzzing sound, and spiky fur grew all over his body.

After trying to transform himself one last time, Andre came out looking even more hideous. He could not bear to look at himself. Finally, Andre asked Helene to kill him and, with great sadness, she agreed.

When I had finished reading the confession, I looked at Helene and told her that I understood what she had done. Then I showed the note to the police inspector. Together, we decided never to speak of it again.

At my brother's funeral, I heard a strange buzzing noise. I looked around for a fly with a white head and arms but could not see anything. I still look out for that fly, wondering if part of Andre is out there, somewhere....

THE END

CREATING THE CREATURE

George Langelaan

George Langelaan

George Langelaan was born on 19 January 1908, in Paris, France. His father was British and his mother was French. He worked as a news reporter in the 1930s, and during World War II he worked as a spy.

Langelaan was known for writing short science-fiction stories, including *The Fly*, which was published in 1957. The story became so popular that it was later turned into a movie. His other well-known stories include *The Lady From Nowhere*, *The Other Hand* and *Cold Blood*. Langelaan's stories are very good at making us think about what it is to be human.

One of the biggest influences in his writing was the famous American author, Edgar Allan Poe, with whom Langelaan shared a birthday. George Langelaan died in 1969.

The Fly (1958)

How it all began... The Fly

"I have always feared any type of bell ring. Even during the day in my office, I answer the phone but I can't help being sickened by the sound of it ringing. But during the night, especially when it surprises me while I'm sleeping, the phone's ring unleashes an animal-like panic in me. I then need to get myself in control before I'm able to even move to turn on the light and get up to answer the phone. Even then I need to make a huge effort to speak with a calm voice. I cannot go back to my normal state of being until I recognize the voice that is addressing me from the other side of the phone line, and I do not feel completely at peace until I know what it's all about."

Edgar Allan Poe

During his life, Edgar Allan Poe wrote a lot of poetry and became known as a master of the short story, particularly the horror story.

Poe will always be remembered for his scary tales, such as *The Black Cat*, *The Oval Portrait*, *The Pit and the Pendulum* and *The Fall of the House of Usher*. He is also known for his poem *The Raven*, his novel *The Narrative of Arthur Gordon Pym* and his tale *The Murders in the Rue Morgue*.

Born in Boston, United States, on 19 January 1809, Poe was an orphan. He was never officially adopted, but a wealthy couple took care of him and made sure he received an education. Poe began to write poetry when he was a teenager.

Edgar Allan Poe

In 1836, he married his cousin, Virginia Eliza Clemm. She died of tuberculosis eleven years later. Two years after that, Poe himself passed away of unknown causes.

Poe is considered a master of crime and mystery stories. Readers of all ages around the world are still terrified when they read his tales.

Virginia Eliza Clemm

This is how Poe's story The Black Cat begins....

"I do not hope nor ask anyone to believe in the simple but strange story that I am about to write. I would be insane if I hoped for that to happen, when my senses reject their own evidence. But I am not crazy and I know for certain that it is not a dream. I am going to die tomorrow and I would like to relieve my soul today. My immediate purpose is to tell, simply and succinctly, a series of domestic events. The consequence of these events has terrified me, they have tortured me, and finally they have destroyed me."

STRANGE BUT TRUE

Did you know that the common housefly has been known to carry over 100 different kinds of disease-causing germs? Now that's gruesome!

Hybrid creatures such as The Fly, which are mixes of different types of animals and people, have long been part of mythology and legend. The Centaur (part-man, part-horse), the Minotaur (part-man, part-bull) and the sphinx (part-man, part-lion) are some famous examples.

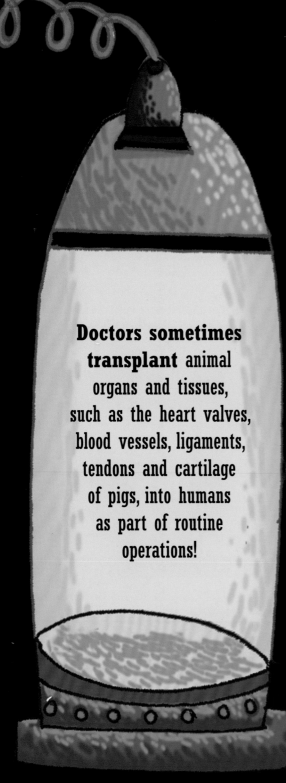

Doctors sometimes transplant animal organs and tissues, such as the heart valves, blood vessels, ligaments, tendons and cartilage of pigs, into humans as part of routine operations!

$B = (A_n)^2 \times \left| \frac{c}{1} \right| + A^2\%$

$\sqrt{} Z^2 =$

$(\cdot \frac{1}{8}) 280$

$\times \frac{30}{3})2\sqrt{\frac{8}{2}}$

THE AMAZING FACTS

Science can change the way we think about things.

ALBERT EINSTEIN

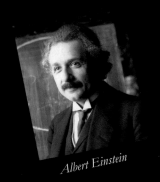
Albert Einstein

Born in Germany on 14 March 1879, Einstein is famous for his theory of relativity, which made us all think differently about time and space. His ideas have inspired many science fiction writers. Einstein is considered the most important scientist of the 20th century. In 1921, he won the Nobel Prize for Physics.

Einstein was also known for his strong belief in world peace. He encouraged other scientists to join together to rid the world of nuclear weapons. Einstein spent his later years teaching in the United States. He died on 18 April 1955, at the age of 76.

$$E = mc^2$$

THE NOBEL PRIZE

The Nobel Prize was named after Alfred Nobel, who invented the explosives dynamite and gelignite. This famous prize is awarded to people who have made an important discovery or a great contribution to Physics, Chemistry, Literature, Peace or Medicine.

TELEPORTATION

In science fiction, teleportation is used to make objects or bodies disintegrate, then reappear in a different place. The characters below have all used or experimented with teleportation at one time or another.

The Man without a Body

Written by Edgar Page Mitchell in 1877, this story is about a scientist who finds a way to disintegrate the atoms of a cat and send them through a telegraph cable. When he tries to do it with his own body, the telegraph runs out of power, teleporting only his head!

The Disintegration Machine

This tale, written by Arthur Conan Doyle in 1929, tells the story of an inventor who builds a machine that disintegrates objects and puts them back together again. The machine becomes a powerful weapon.

Star Trek

Created by Gene Roddenberry, this popular television show first appeared in September 1966. It tells the adventures of the crew of the starship *Enterprise*. They journey to unknown worlds and discover new civilizations. In the spaceship, there is a transporter that teleports people from the ship to the surfaces of new planets.

Nightcrawler

This character from the comic book *X-Men* is a mutant who can teleport from one place to another. When he teleports, he leaves behind a smelly smoke. The X-Men were created by Stan Lee and Jack Kirby and first appeared in 1963.

Goku

Goku is a character from the Japanese *Dragon Ball* series created by Akira Toriyama. This manga comic book series has been made into animated films. Goku is able to use teleportation.

Hiro Nakamura

This popular character from the TV series *Heroes* can teleport himself to any time or place. He can travel great distances, and is able to stop time or make it pass more slowly. The first season of *Heroes was shown in 2006.*

THE LABORATORY

How do magnets work?

You will need:
- A magnet
- A steel fork
- A steel spoon
- Other steel objects: clips, lids or hooks

Keep magnets away from magnetic media, such as televisions, credit cards and cassette tapes.

1 Rub the fork against the magnet for one minute, always in the same direction.

2 Hold the fork near the other steel objects. Notice what happens.

3 Now place the magnet on the metal handle of the spoon.

4 Try putting the spoon near the other metallic objects. Notice what happens to those objects.

What happened?
The fork and spoon became magnets themselves. This happens when a magnet is stuck to a steel object or if the steel object is stroked with a magnet. If the steel objects are dropped or hit, they will stop being magnetic.

The sun's heat

You will need:
- A sheet of white paper
- A sheet of black paper
- Water
- Two glasses
- Sticky tape
- Scissors

Be careful when using scissors!

1 Cut a piece of white paper to wrap around the outside of one of the glasses. Wrap the paper around the glass and secure it with tape.

2 Repeat step 1 using black paper and the other glass.

3 Pour the same amount of water into both glasses.

4 Use the leftover white paper to make a lid for the white glass. Use the leftover black paper to make a lid for the black glass.

5 Place both glasses in the sunlight. Wait for a few hours, then take off the lids. Test the water in each glass with your finger. What do you notice?

What happened?
The water in the black glass should have been warmer than the water in the white glass. This is because the white paper reflected light, while the black paper absorbed light and heated the water.

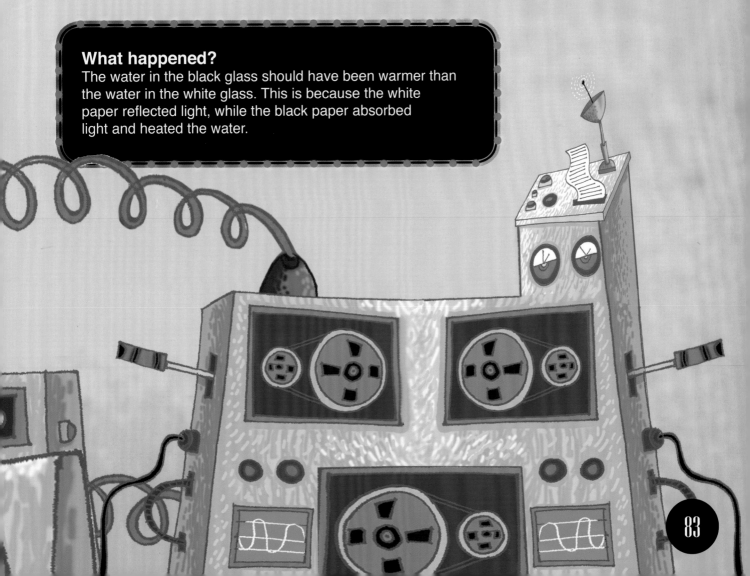

THE CREATURE FROM THE BLACK LAGOON

THE STORY OF THE MOVIE

During a journey to the Amazon Jungle, a scientist named Doctor Carl Maia made an amazing discovery. He found a fossil showing the remains of an ancient and extraordinary creature! Doctor Maia knew there would be more fossils nearby, but he would need help finding them. He left his camp and travelled home to gather a team together.

At home, Doctor Maia invited several scientists
to help him. He also asked his friend, David Reed, who
was an expert on fossils, to join the team. But Doctor Maia
was not happy when David brought along his girlfriend, Kay, too.
Kay was not a scientist and had not done much travelling before.

The team's journey was long and filled with danger. After crossing the stormy
ocean by ship, they travelled along the murky Amazon River. Then they
walked deep into the jungle, carefully avoiding poisonous snakes and frogs.

Finally, the group reached a small clearing by the edge of a lake, where Doctor
Maia had left his camp. But as soon as the doctor arrived, he realized
something was wrong. His camp had been destroyed!

The scientists decided a wild animal must be to blame and didn't make much
of it. They tidied the camp, put up new tents and started their work. They
were all eager to find the fossils that showed the rest of the creature's skeleton.

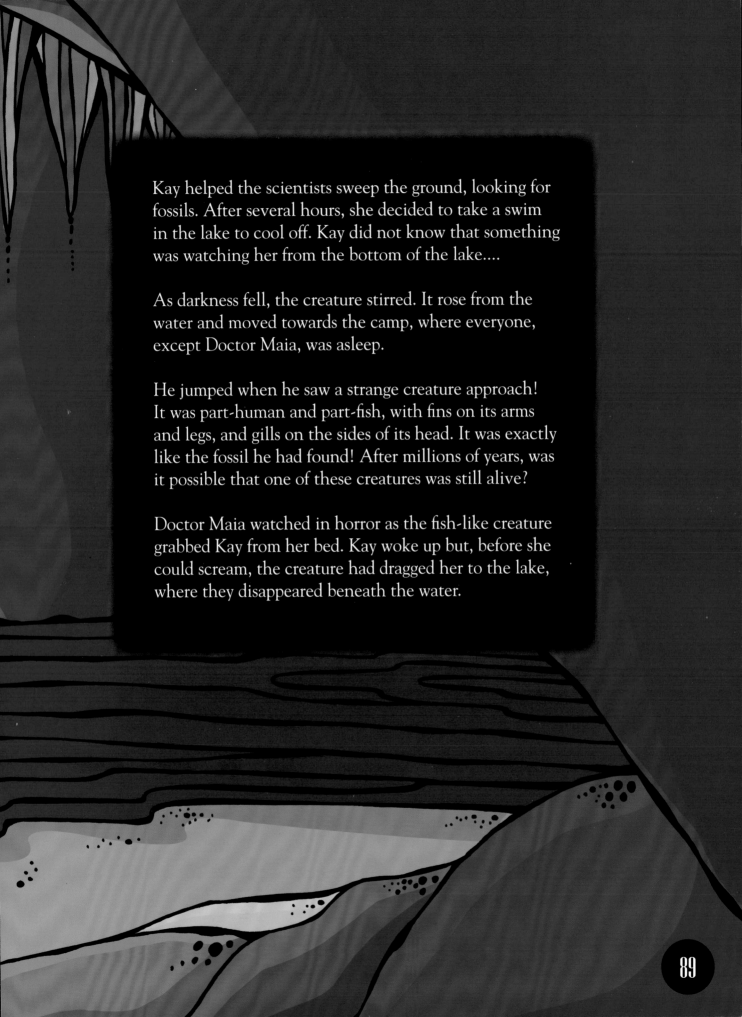

Kay helped the scientists sweep the ground, looking for fossils. After several hours, she decided to take a swim in the lake to cool off. Kay did not know that something was watching her from the bottom of the lake....

As darkness fell, the creature stirred. It rose from the water and moved towards the camp, where everyone, except Doctor Maia, was asleep.

He jumped when he saw a strange creature approach! It was part-human and part-fish, with fins on its arms and legs, and gills on the sides of its head. It was exactly like the fossil he had found! After millions of years, was it possible that one of these creatures was still alive?

Doctor Maia watched in horror as the fish-like creature grabbed Kay from her bed. Kay woke up but, before she could scream, the creature had dragged her to the lake, where they disappeared beneath the water.

Doctor Maia woke the other scientists at once, and explained what had happened. They must rescue Kay from this dreadful creature! The scientists gathered spears and nets, and waded into the lake. In the darkness of night, it looked like a deep, black lagoon.

After several hours, they finally found Kay. She was lying very still on a grassy mound, above the water's surface. She must have escaped! As the scientists reached out for Kay, the huge creature suddenly burst from the water, roaring with rage.

Kay screamed in terror! Her fright startled the creature and, quick as a flash, the scientists threw their spears, piercing the creature in the chest. With a shriek, the creature fell back into the black lake.

Kay was rescued and Doctor Maia agreed that everyone should leave the camp. Together, they returned home, and no one ever saw or heard of the creature again.

STRANGE BUT TRUE

Many real-life monsters living in the Amazon River are an actual deadly threat to humans, such as the fresh-water stingray, the electric eel, the caiman (a member of the alligator family) and meat-eating piranha fish. Keep out!

The Creature from the Black Lagoon has relatives alive today. One of these is the Snakehead Fish, which can grow more than 1 metre in length and can live on land as well as in the water. This fish also goes by the impressive name 'Fishzilla'.

The Creature from the Black Lagoon is not the only underwater creature to have struck fear in people. In the past, sailors were very afraid of seeing a mermaid while at sea, as mermaids were thought to bring disaster!

THE DEEP, DARK FACTS

Diving

People have always been interested in what lies beneath rivers, lakes and oceans. But humans cannot survive naturally underwater. For thousands of years, people could only explore beneath the water's surface by holding their breath – which didn't get them very far!

In the middle of the 20th century, a scientist called Émile Gagnan and an explorer named Jacques-Yves Cousteau created important diving equipment.

They made a special face mask, called a regulator, which was attached to a tank full of air. The regulator allowed people to breathe underwater. Divers could safely stay underwater for longer than ever before.

Émile Gagnan
(1900–1979)

Born in France, this engineer later moved to Canada and set up a laboratory where he could design and test diving equipment.

Jacques-Yves Cousteau
(1910–1997)

Known as 'Captain Cousteau', this man was an explorer who studied underwater creatures and the environment. He worked with Gagnan to make the diving regulator.

Diving equipment

Here's a quick guide to the equipment used by divers to help them make the most of their time underwater.

Ballast belt: This special belt contains weights to help a diver stay underwater.

BCD jacket: This jacket has an air chamber that helps a diver float on the water's surface. The amount of air in the chamber can be changed to allow the diver to swim underwater.

Boots: These protect a diver's feet from the cold water.

Watch: A watch shows divers how long they have spent underwater.

Flippers: Flippers make it easier to swim faster, making sure the diver's legs don't get tired too quickly. Flippers can be worn with or without diving boots.

Gauge: This shows divers how much air is left in their tanks.

Mask or visor: The diver wears a mask or visor to protect their eyes, allowing them to see underwater.

Nozzle: At the end of a tube, this spout is used to breathe through.

Regulator: This controls the flow of air so a diver can breathe safely underwater.

Snorkel: A snorkel allows divers to breathe near the water's surface.

Tank: This contains air, allowing the diver to breathe underwater. The tank is attached to the diver by a harness.

Wetsuit: A wetsuit is a tight suit worn by divers to stop their bodies from getting too cold in the water.

Make an origami boat

What do you need?
- A square piece of paper measuring at least 20 centimetres across
- A table or flat surface

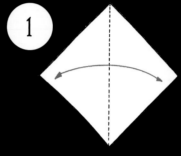

1

Fold your piece of paper in half diagonally and open it out. You will need this crease later.

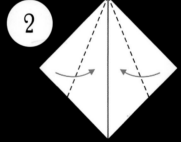

2

Fold two sides of the square inwards, toward the crease. This makes two flaps. Look at the dotted lines in this picture to help you.

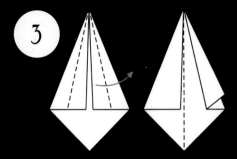

3

Fold each flap outwards again, using these pictures to guide you.

4

Pick up your paper and fold it in half, along the crease in the centre, with the flaps on the outside. Now fold the bottom part upwards, using this picture to help you.

5

Unfold the bottom part so it is pointing downwards again.

6

Take the bottom part in both hands and turn it inside out. You'll need to open out your boat to do this. Your boat should now stand upright on a table.

KING KONG

THE STORY OF THE MOVIE

Ann Darrow was a beautiful girl from New York who wanted to be a famous actress. Ann's beauty attracted the attention of Carl Denham, a director who was about to make an extraordinary movie.

Carl asked Ann to be in the movie. But he hadn't yet decided where his film would be made. Then Carl found an old map that showed a mysterious place called Skull Island.

Carl and his film crew set off for the mysterious island by sea. Their journey lasted several weeks, and Ann became friends with an actor called Jack Driscoll.

When their ship arrived at Skull Island, the crew discovered a place covered with thick tropical jungle. Many dinosaurs, prehistoric beasts and ancient tribes were living there. Before long, Ann was captured by one of the tribes. They dragged her away, tied her up and left her in a wide, open space. Ann was about to be killed!

Suddenly, Ann heard something storming through the forest. Standing before her was a giant gorilla: Kong. Ann was terrified! Kong stood over her and broke the chains around her ankles. He stretched out a huge hand, scooped her up and carried her into the jungle.

Jack, Carl and the others saw what happened and decided to rescue Ann from the beast. They did not know that Kong was a gentle giant. He didn't want to hurt Ann; he just wanted her company.

Once Kong arrived at his cave, he carefully placed Ann on the floor. Ann realized that he meant her no harm and she simply curled up and fell fast asleep.

At dawn, Kong went to look for food. He left Ann hidden in the branches of a tall tree. Suddenly, a terrifying dinosaur came running through the forest straight towards Ann.

Kong ran back to Ann, hit the dinosaur and knocked him down. The dinosaur stood up and roared in anger, but Kong was ready to fight.

Jack and the others heard the vicious battle. But while Jack planned to rescue Ann, Carl had his own ideas. He wanted to capture Kong. He thought people back at home would flock to see the giant beast, and that would make Carl rich and famous.

While Kong was fighting the dinosaur, Jack helped Ann to climb down from the tree. They set off together to a nearby village, hearing Kong roar in victory as he defeated the dinosaur. When Kong realized that Ann had gone, he stormed after her. Carl and the sailors attacked the beast with sleeping gas. They carried Kong to the ship, and headed back to the United States.

Several weeks later, Carl announced a new show that promised to be the greatest show New York City had ever seen. The opening day arrived, and the theatre was full. The curtains opened to reveal the huge gorilla, held down by thick chains. Carl introduced him as "King Kong: The Eighth Wonder of the World!".

People began to take pictures, but the camera flashes upset Kong. He roared in anger, broke his chains and knocked down the walls of the theatre. Everyone in the audience panicked and ran to escape Kong's fury. Kong destroyed everything in his way. He wanted to find his friend, Ann.

104

Suddenly, a group of planes flew above them. The planes had been sent to destroy Kong! The giant gorilla gently placed Ann down and turned towards the planes. They started shooting at Kong. He swiped at them but was wounded and fell from the building. The ground shook when the huge creature hit the street below.

Ann was rescued and joined the crowd that had gathered to gaze at Kong's lifeless body. Ann felt sad. She knew that Kong had never meant her any harm. Finally, Ann was reunited with Jack. But she never forgot Kong, the gentle giant.

Ann knew she was the only one who could stop Kong. She called to the beast to calm him.

When he heard Ann's voice, Kong took her in his hands and ran through the city. He climbed to the top of the Empire State Building, where he thought he would be safe. Ann was not afraid. She knew that Kong would protect her.

THE END

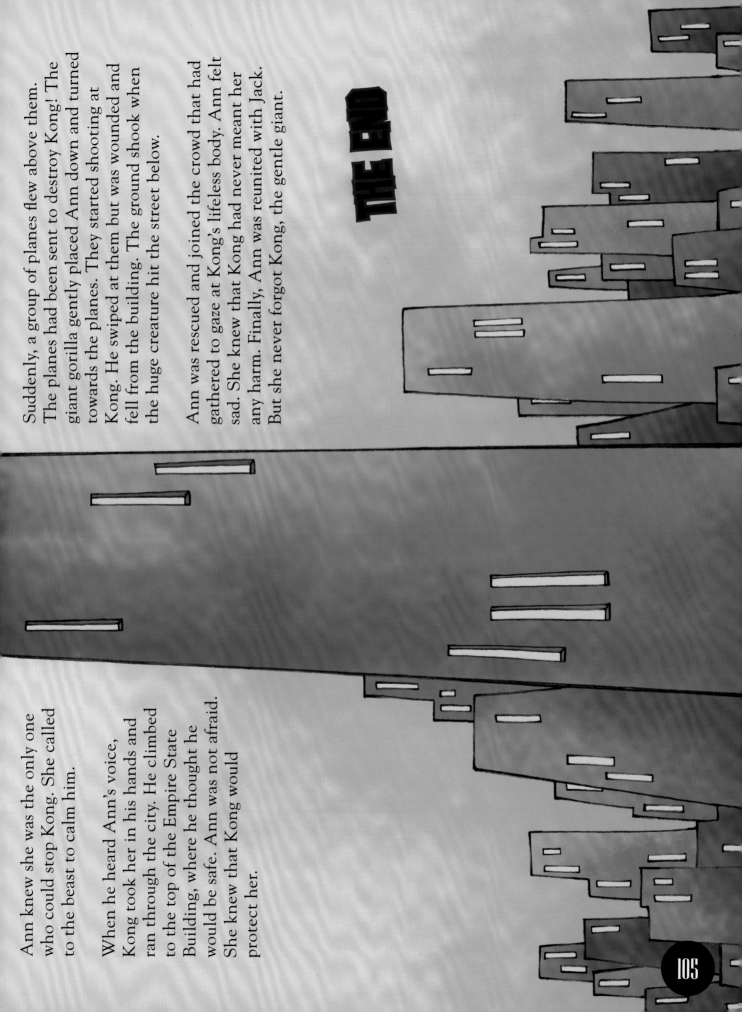

CREATING THE CREATURE

Merian C. Cooper

Merian C. Cooper was born on 24 October 1893, and died on 21 April 1973. He was a director, producer and screenwriter, but also a keen aviator and Air Force officer. Cooper worked for several years in film production companies, before moving to Metro Goldwyn Mayer, or MGM.

Cooper brought *King Kong* to life for the first time, working with Ernest B. Schoedsack to develop the movie. *King Kong* was shown to an audience for the first time in 1933. Almost all of the movie was filmed inside a studio.

On the left, Merian C. Cooper

Willis O'Brien was in charge of special effects for *King Kong* and won many awards for his work. He used miniature models and the sounds of real wild animals to try to make Skull Island a believable place.

Willis O'Brien with a model of Kong

Merian C. Cooper and Ernest B. Schoedsack

King Kong is considered a classic movie masterpiece. It has become a symbol that represents modern popular culture. Kong is considered one of the most famous monsters in history.

King Kong Characteristics

Scientific name: *Gigantopithecus*
Common name: King Kong
Place of birth: Skull Island
Height: 45 metres
Weight: 2 tonnes

Talents: Strength, intelligence, compassion
Rivals: Godzilla

King Kong on TV

Kong had his own cartoon series between 1966 and 1969, called *The King Kong Show*. The series had three seasons with a total of 25 episodes. The story focussed on the huge gorilla and his relationship with the Bond family.

Kong: The Animated Series was another animated series for children. It was created in 2001 and ran until 2006, with a total of 40 episodes. The story focussed on the cloning of King Kong.

STRANGE BUT TRUE

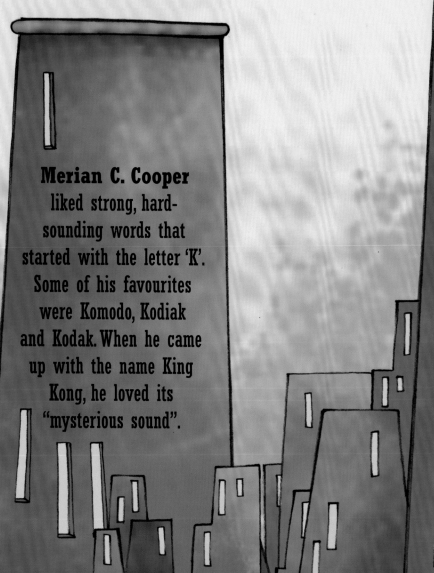

Merian C. Cooper liked strong, hard-sounding words that started with the letter 'K'. Some of his favourites were Komodo, Kodiak and Kodak. When he came up with the name King Kong, he loved its "mysterious sound".

The largest ape ever to walk the Earth was Gigantopithecus, who lived hundreds of thousands of years ago. Fossils suggest that the creature would have stood up to 3 metres tall, and weighed up to 550 kilograms — even bigger than Bigfoot!

Merian C. Cooper said that he got the idea for a King Kong movie after dreaming that a giant gorilla was terrorizing New York City. He combined this dream with stories his friends told him about exotic travelling adventures.

THE FEARSOME FACTS

Giant mammals

King Kong is a make-believe giant gorilla from a story, but some very large mammals are not imaginary at all!

The Polar Bear
The polar bear is the largest hunter on land. It can grow up to 3 metres long and weighs over a tonne. Polar bears live in the icy regions of the northern hemisphere, where they hunt for seals.

The Hippopotamus
The largest recorded hippo was nearly 5 tonnes in weight, 5 metres long, and over 1.5 metres tall. Hippos usually have short legs and a barrel-shaped body. They also have large heads and wide mouths.

The Blue Whale

The blue whale is the largest animal in the world. This giant sea mammal can reach up to 30 metres in length and weigh in at around 200 tonnes.

The blue whale has no known predators due to its enormous size, strength and speed. However, it is in serious danger of becoming extinct because it has been hunted by humans in the past.

The African Elephant

The African elephant is the largest mammal on land. It can measure up to 4 metres in height, and can weigh over 6 tonnes. It has a large head and huge ears that cover its shoulders. An elephant has a long trunk and two tusks in its upper jaw.

Elephants walk on land at speeds of just under 6.5 kilometres per hour, but can run at up to 40 kilometres per hour when frightened.

The White Rhinoceros

The white rhinoceros lives in Africa and grows to almost 5 metres in length. It stands at well over 2 metres tall, and weighs about 2-4 tonnes. It has two horns made of keratin, which is similar to the material our fingernails are made from. If a rhino breaks a horn, it can grow it back, growing at a rate of nearly 8 centimetres per year. Rhinos are currently threatened by hunters who kill them for their valuable horns.

The Giraffe

The giraffe is the tallest land-living animal. It uses its long neck to reach leaves growing high up in the trees. Giraffes can grow up to 6 metres tall and weigh around 2 tonnes. Giraffes are usually found in the grasslands of Africa.

THE LABORATORY

Melting ice

What do you need?
- Three dishes
- Three ice cubes
- Salt
- Sugar

1 Place one of the ice cubes in a dish. Add some salt.

2 Place a second ice cube in a separate dish. Add some sugar.

3 Place the last ice cube in the third dish on it Which ice cubes melt the fastest?

What happened?
The ice cubes placed with the sa
and sugar melted faster. Ice cube
have a layer of liquid water on the
surface. This layer was disturbed
by the salt and sugar so that the
melted faster.

Fresh water and salt water

What do you need?
- A glass
- Tap water
- Artificial colouring
- An ice cube tray
- A freezer compartment
- A tablespoon
- Salt

1 Fill the glass with tap water and add some artificial colouring. Slowly pour the mixture into the ice cube tray. Place it carefully in the freezer. Leave it there overnight, or until the ice cubes are solid.

2 Refill the glass with water. This time, add two or three tablespoons of salt. Stir the mixture until the salt has dissolved.

3 Remove two or three ice cubes and put them into the glass of salt water. Wait a few seconds and see what happens.

What happened?
As the ice cubes melted, the fresh water with the colouring stayed on the surface. It didn't dissolve into the salt water and appeared to be 'floating' on top. This is because fresh water is less dense than salt water.

The Phantom
of the Opera

Original story by Gaston Leroux

Christine was a beautiful young singer. She had been chosen from dozens of talented singers to perform at the famous Opera House in Paris. The Opera House was a wonderful theatre, but it was also home to a terrible ghost – the Phantom of the Opera.

Every night, Christine performed in front of a large audience at the Opera House. People came from all over the world to hear her sing. A masked figure also watched from the shadows. It was the Phantom!

One evening, tragedy struck. The rope holding the huge chandelier hanging from the ceiling of the Opera House was mysteriously cut, and the chandelier crashed into the audience below! Everyone fled in panic.

Christine rushed back to her dressing room where the Phantom suddenly appeared. He sprayed Christine with a gas that made her fall into a deep sleep. Then, he carried Christine down a long, dark staircase, far beneath the theatre.

Finally, they came to an underground lake where the Phantom had a boat waiting. He carried Christine onto the boat, and they crossed the lake to his secret hideout.

When Christine awoke, the masked Phantom explained that he was not really a ghost, but a man named Erik. He told Christine that he was deeply in love with her and was willing to do anything to make her happy.

Christine was so shocked that she fainted!

She woke up in a strange room. The Phantom had left a note saying that she was free to leave and return whenever she wished.

Just then, Christine heard a beautiful voice coming from the next room. She walked toward the music and, to her surprise, found the Phantom singing and playing an organ.

Christine moved closer to the Phantom. She wanted to see what he really looked like. Gently, she touched his mask. The mask slipped away to reveal an ugly, deformed face. Christine shrieked!

This made Erik very angry. He told Christine that she was now his prisoner. Christine cried, begging him to change his mind. Finally, the Phantom forced her to make a promise – she could leave him once, for a short time, then she must return and stay with him forever.

The Phantom released Christine and she hurried back to the theatre to find her friend, Raoul. She quickly explained how she had been taken by the Phantom and that she had to return to him. Raoul promised to keep her safe and, together, they planned to leave the city.

The Phantom had been spying on the two friends. When he heard their plan, he told Christine that she must leave with him immediately, or he would destroy the theatre! Sadly, Christine agreed. She followed the Phantom to a carriage outside the Opera House.

Raoul ran after them, shouting to everyone in the street that the Phantom of the Opera was alive and had to be stopped. A large group of people crowded around the carriage, shaking it. The carriage toppled over and Christine was thrown to the ground.

While everyone turned to help Christine, the Phantom escaped. He leapt off a nearby bridge into the murky waters below. His mask floated slowly to the surface. The Phantom of the Opera was never seen again.

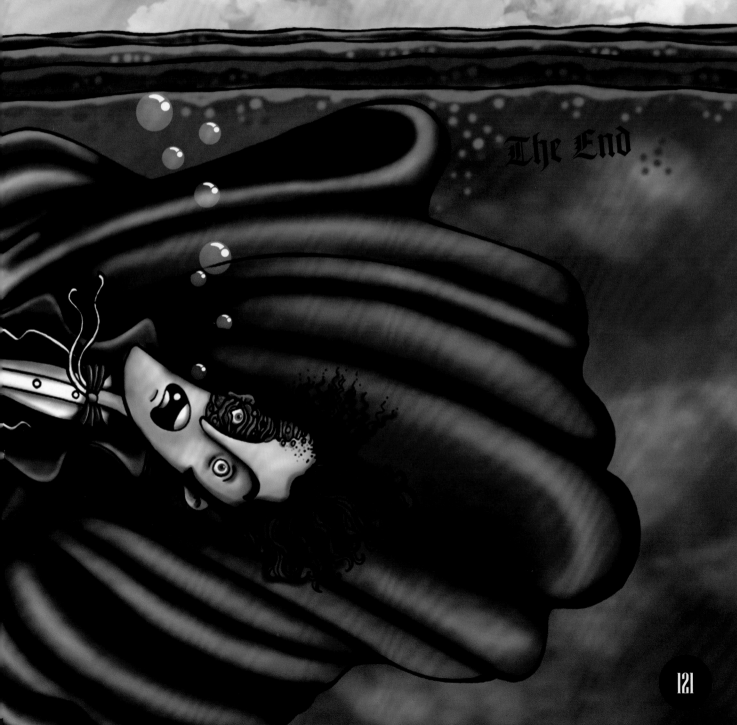

The End

CREATING THE CREATURE

Gaston Louis Alfred Leroux

Gaston Louis Alfred Leroux was born in Paris, France, on 6 May 1868. He studied law and graduated in 1889 to become a lawyer. After several years, Leroux changed careers and began working as a newspaper journalist.

In 1907, Leroux wrote a detective story called *Mystery of the Yellow Room*, which was a great success. He also wrote novels, such as *The Perfume of the Lady in Black*. In 1909, Leroux stopped working as a journalist and dedicated his life to writing fiction. His most famous work was *The Phantom of The Opera*.

Leroux died at the age of 56 in Niza, France, on 15 April 1927.

Gaston Louis Alfred Leroux

How he created the Phantom of the Opera

The Phantom of the Opera combines romance, terror, mystery and tragedy. It tells the story of a mysterious man who haunted the Paris Opera House, trying to make a young girl fall in love with him. The story has since been adapted for movies, the theatre and television.

The Eiffel Tower, Paris

Man or Phantom?

The main character in Leroux's story is called Erik. He is the son of a stonework teacher. Erik was born with a deformed face which shocked and scared his parents. Their lack of love forced Erik to run away. He hid beneath the Opera House in Paris, sometimes watching the operas. So that people would not be frightened by his face, Erik started wearing a mask. Soon, he became known as 'the Phantom of the Opera'.

Phantom Musicals

Ken Hill (1937–1995) wrote plays and adapted many stories to make them suitable for the theatre. These included *The Phantom of the Opera*, *The Curse of The Werewolf* and *The Invisible Man*.

Andrew Lloyd Webber later set the story of *The Phantom of the Opera* to music, and it became one of the best-selling musicals of all time.

Extract from The Phantom of the Opera

"The Phantom of the Opera really existed. He was not, as was long believed, a creature of the imagination of the artists, the superstition of the managers, or a product of the absurd and impressionable brains of the young ladies of the ballet, their mothers, the box-keepers, the cloak-room attendants or the concierge. Yes, he existed in flesh and blood, although he had the complete appearance of a phantom; that is to say, of a ghostly shadow."

THE PHANTOM FACTS

The Opera

An opera is a musical performance where singers and musicians act out a dramatic play. Operas combine words with music and are usually performed on the stage of a theatre.

Operas are, in many ways, similar to normal plays. They use acting, scenery, costumes and sometimes dancing to tell a story.

Origins

The word 'opera' comes from the Latin word *opus*, meaning 'work' or 'labour'. Operas began in Italy in the late 16th century.

The first opera was called *Dafne* and was written by Jacopo Peri. It was composed in 1597 in Florence, Italy. Unfortunately, all copies of *Dafne* have been lost, but a later work by Peri, called *Euridice,* has survived.

One early work that is still performed today is *L'Orfeo*. This was written in 1607 by the Italian composer, Claudio Monteverdi.

Claudio Monteverdi   Wolfgang Amadeus Mozart   Henry Purcell   Faustina Bordoni

Famous Composers

Many of the world's greatest composers have written operas. These include the English composer Henry Purcell, who wrote *Dido and Aeneas* around 1689.

Later, the German composer George Frederic Handel composed several operas while he lived in London. These include *Ariodante* and *Alcina*.

One of the greatest composers of opera was Wolfgang Amadeus Mozart. In total, Mozart wrote more than 600 pieces of music, including more than 20 operas. They include *Die Zauberflöte* (*The Magic Flute*) and *Le Nozze de Figaro* (*The Marriage of Figaro*).

During the 19th century, the great Italian composer Giuseppe Verdi wrote more than 30 operas. Meanwhile, German composer Richard Wagner wrote grand operas using stories from myths and legends. Several of these are still performed today.

Composers of opera from the 20th century include the Russian Igor Stravinsky and the Austrian-American Arnold Schoenberg.

Voices in the Opera

Opera singers are separated into different groups, depending on how high or low they can make their voices when they sing.

Male singers are divided into bass, bass-baritone, tenor or countertenor.

Female singers are divided into contralto, mezzo-soprano and soprano. One famous female singer was Faustina Bordoni. She was a mezzo-soprano in the 18th century.

Other famous opera singers include Maria Callas, Enrico Caruso, Montserrat Caballé, Rosa Ponselle, Luciano Pavarotti, Plácido Domingo and Jose Carreras.

Enrico Caruso   Giuseppe Verdi   Farinelli   Igor Stravinsky   Montserrat Caballé

THE LABORATORY

What do you need?
• A medium-sized balloon
• Newspaper, torn into strips
• Glue mixed with water
• A marker pen
• Scissors
• Paints and a paintbrush
• A length of elastic

Ask an adult to help you.

Make the phantom's mask

1 Inflate the balloon and tie a knot in it.

2 Wet each strip of newspaper with glue and stick it to the balloon. Continue doing this until the balloon is covered with at least four layers of newspaper. This is called papier mâché.

3 Leave the balloon to dry for 24 hours. Then ask an adult to pop the balloon.

4 Use the marker pen to draw two eyes, eyebrows and a nose onto your papier mâché model. The pointed part of your model should be pointing downward, like a chin.

5 Ask an adult to cut out the eyes. Then cut the mask in half horizontally, beneath the nose. Also cut away the back half of the mask. Finally paint your mask.

6 When the mask is dry, ask an adult to pierce a hole at each side of the mask and tie a piece of elastic through the holes. Now you are ready to become the Phantom of the Opera!

The WAR of the WORLDS

Original story by H. G. Wells

One night, a famous scientist named Ogilvy invited some friends to his home in England. Ogilvy and his friends were experts in astronomy – they knew all about space and the planets.

While the scientists were looking through Ogilvy's powerful telescopes, they saw strange green lights in the sky. At first, they thought the lights were space rocks, or meteors. Suddenly, one of the rocks appeared to zoom towards Earth, landing in a nearby field! The scientists set off to find it.

To their surprise, instead of a space rock, the scientists found a strange cylinder nearly 30 metres long. Before long, other cylinders were landing all over the country. They weren't meteors. They were strange spaceships, full of Martians! Earth had been invaded!

The Martians crawled out from their spaceships. They had large, round bodies with long, thick tentacles. As they moved along the ground, they used their tentacles to push anything and anyone in their path out of the way.

The Martians began to make huge three-legged machines, called Tripods. Each Tripod gave out a scorching ray of heat and a cloud of black smoke that was poisonous to humans.

The Martians and their Tripods travelled towards London, destroying everything in their way. Giant clouds of the evil black smoke followed them.

London was in chaos! People fled from their homes, trying to hide. They knew if the Martians found them, they would be killed.

Finally, the British army was ordered to fight back against the Martians. They shot at the Martians, and when they managed to hit one, it collapsed with steam and green slime oozing from its insides.

But the Martians were too strong for the army. They would not back down, and they could not be beaten. London was soon covered in thick, black smoke. Before long, the city was deserted.

133

But gradually, some of the Martians got weaker. Then they grew so weak that they died. The scientists realized that the Martians were being attacked by germs and viruses, such as the common cold.

Humans fight these germs from the moment we are born, but the Martians were not used to them. Their bodies did not know how to fight illness.

One by one, the Martians became ill, and began dropping like flies. Finally, they were all dead. The black smoke cleared, and people moved back to their homes.

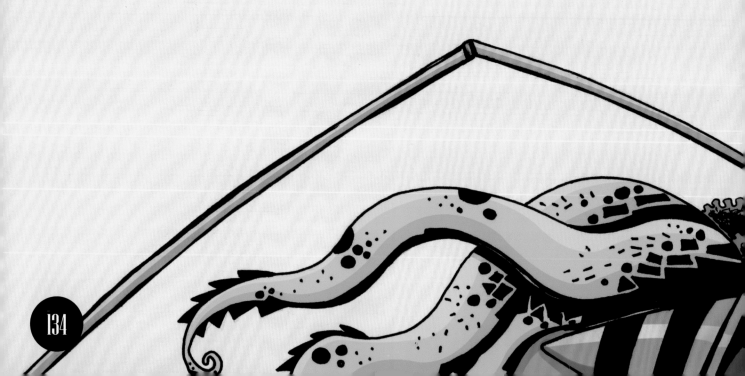

From then on, Ogilvy and his friends used telescopes to watch the sky very closely. The Martians' landing had proved there were other life forms out there. But what other creatures lived in space? Could there be other aliens plotting a similar invasion?

Planet Earth was safe for now. Until the next time....

The End

CREATING THE CREATURE

H. G. Wells

Herbert George Wells was born on 21 September 1866, in the United Kingdom. He was the fourth child of Joseph Wells and Sarah Neal. When he was young, Herbert had an accident that meant he spent a long time in bed, recovering. This is when his love of books began – books were Herbert's way of escaping the boredom of his bedroom.

Herbert did very well at school. Later, he was awarded a degree in zoology from the University of London. He also studied geology, learning about materials that make up the Earth. Herbert went on to become a science teacher.

Herbert George Wells

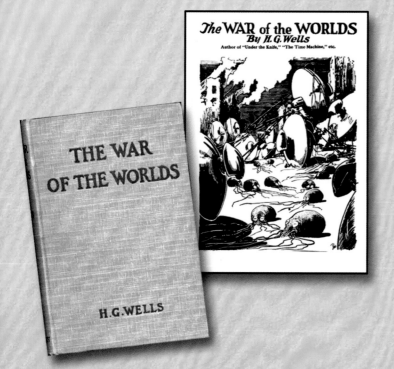

Under the name H. G. Wells, Herbert wrote many stories, including *The Time Machine*, *The Island of Doctor Moreau*, *The Invisible Man* and *The War of the Worlds*. He died on 13 August 1946. H. G. Wells was added to the Science Fiction Hall of Fame, because of his great work.

The War of the Worlds, published in 1898, was the first book to describe an alien invasion on Earth. Since then, there have been many versions of this story in movies, radio, television and comics.

Is Earth Under Attack?

On 30 October 1938, a radio station in the United States introduced a new show and then began playing a special radio version of *The War of the Worlds* story. Unfortunately, many listeners had not heard the introduction.

Radio listeners heard only that a large, unknown object had fallen from the sky on the outskirts of New Jersey. The large object was then described as a spaceship full of aliens! There were reports that the invaders were heading for New York.

Hundreds of people thought the alien invasion was real! They began to leave their homes, in search of safety. Minutes later, it became clear that the story on the radio was not real. The story's narrator, Orson Welles, had to apologize to the listeners!

Orson Welles speaking on the radio

We Heard Strange Voices....

A similar story happened in Ecuador, South America, where a radio station became famous when it put on a play based on *The War of the Worlds* in 1949.

Radio listeners heard an urgent message that a flying saucer had been seen from the Galapagos Islands, and had fallen on the outskirts of Ecuador's capital city, Quito. Strange voices warned listeners of an alien invasion. They also warned that a cloud of poisonous gas was approaching the city's downtown area. There were orders for the army to defend the city.

The broadcast lasted only 20 minutes, but it had radio listeners on the edge of their seats. People began to flee their homes in fright! But when they realized they had been tricked, the crowds grew angry.

They began to attack the local newspaper office, where the radio station was based. They set newspapers on fire and threw them at the office. Sadly, as the building burned, at least six people were killed.

A passage from The War of the Worlds

"By day, we are so busy in our little affairs, it seems impossible that someone up there watches our steps, and has a careful and detailed plan to conquer Earth. Only the night, with its darkness and silence, creates the right conditions for the Martians and other beings to invade."

STRANGE BUT TRUE

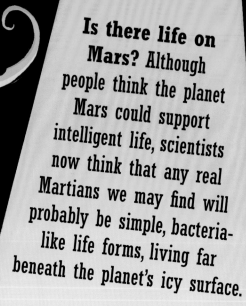

Is there life on Mars? Although people think the planet Mars could support intelligent life, scientists now think that any real Martians we may find will probably be simple, bacteria-like life forms, living far beneath the planet's icy surface.

The term extraterrestrial (another word for alien) is taken from the Latin words 'extra' — meaning 'beyond' or 'not of' — and 'terrestris' — meaning 'of or belonging to Earth'. So aliens are not of Earth!

Human beings have made several attempts to make contact with extraterrestrials, including sending radio messages to distant planets and blasting a DVD with personal messages from 60,000 people into deep space on NASA's Kepler spacecraft in 2009!

In 2010, scientist Stephen Hawking warned that humans should not try to communicate with alien life forms, as they might decide to attack mankind and steal all of the Earth's resources — just like in The War of The Worlds!

THE MYSTERIOUS FACTS

LIFE ON OTHER PLANETS

Humans have always questioned whether we are alone in the Universe. Many people think that the Universe is too large for Earth to be the only planet with living beings.

ALIEN

We use the word 'alien' to describe any living thing that comes from another planet. Many people believe aliens exist, and that they may have already visited Earth. There are many stories from people who say they have seen aliens or spaceships.

According to these people, there are several different types of aliens. These are some of the main ones:

UFO (Unidentified Flying Object)

A UFO is an unknown flying object or machine, thought to come from outer space. There are many stories and recordings from people who think they have seen a UFO.

They describe UFOs that vary in size from small objects able to fly between buildings, to objects so large that they cover whole areas of a city.

They also describe UFOs in a variety of shapes, including disks, spheres, rings and triangles.

The Greys: These are the most common. They are described as being short, with big black eyes, a nose and a mouth. They are small and they don't have hair.

Nordic: These aliens look like human beings. Who knows, aliens could already be living among us!

Zoomorphic: These aliens may look like – or have features similar to – an animal.

CLOSE ENCOUNTERS

A 'close encounter' is the name given to the experience when a person claims to have seen a UFO. There are three different types of close encounter:

A close encounter of the first kind: This is when one or more UFOs are seen in the sky.

A close encounter of the second kind: This is when a UFO is seen and leaves behind some kind of evidence, such as scorch marks in the earth.

Close encounter of the third kind: This is when there is a sighting of both a UFO and the alien operating that UFO.

THE ROSWELL INCIDENT

In July 1947, it was reported that an unidentified object had landed at Roswell in New Mexico, United States. Although first reports said it appeared to be an alien spacecraft, later statements said it was a weather balloon. Some people believe that aliens really did land during the Roswell Incident, and that the government is hiding evidence of this!

AREA 51

Area 51 is a military base for the US Air Force. It can be found about 130 kilometres northwest of Las Vegas. Different types of aircraft are tested here, and new weapons are developed. Some people believe that the technology used in Area 51 comes from outer space, and that the military base is used to store materials and objects from other planets.

ALIEN ABDUCTION

This describes a situation in which one or more aliens kidnaps a human from Earth. Some people claim to have been abducted, and say that the aliens performed experiments on them. Most people believe that these stories are only vivid dreams or strange visions.

THE LABORATORY

Alien noises

What do you need?
- Two balloons
- Water
- A table

Warning! Children under eight years can choke or suffocate on uninflated or broken balloons. Adult supervision required. Keep uninflated balloons from children. Discard broken balloons at once.

1. Blow air into one balloon and tie a knot in it.

2. Fill the other balloon with water and tie a knot in it.

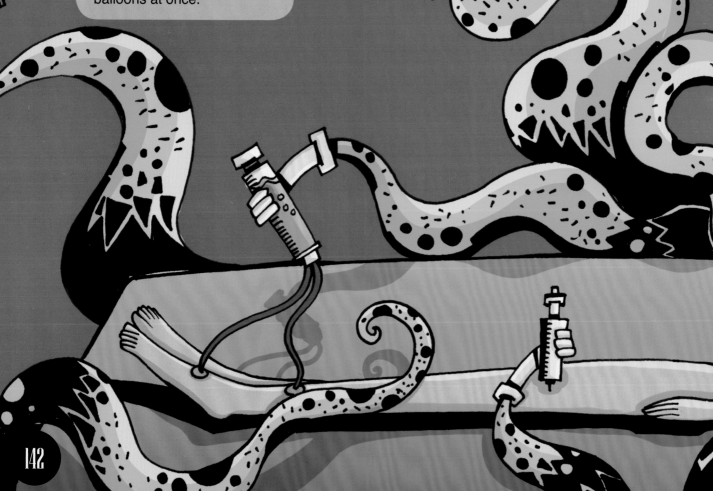

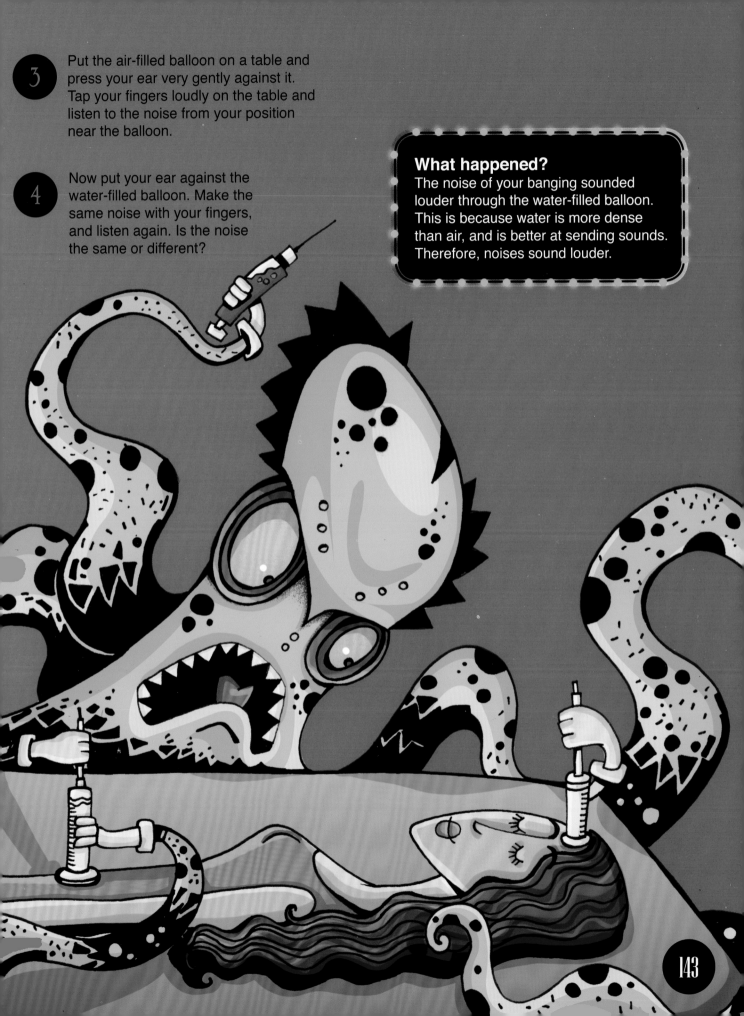

3 Put the air-filled balloon on a table and press your ear very gently against it. Tap your fingers loudly on the table and listen to the noise from your position near the balloon.

4 Now put your ear against the water-filled balloon. Make the same noise with your fingers, and listen again. Is the noise the same or different?

What happened?
The noise of your banging sounded louder through the water-filled balloon. This is because water is more dense than air, and is better at sending sounds. Therefore, noises sound louder.

Godzilla

The story of the movie

This story begins with two fishing boats called *Eiko-Maru* and *Bingo-Maru*. The boats mysteriously disappeared on 8 September 1954, near Odo Island, in Japan. Their logbooks, written by the captains as a record of events, were found the next day.

At 7.30 pm, the captain of the *Eiko-Maru* had written: "There are no fish to catch, and the weather has taken a turn for the worst. We keep hearing strange noises. Conditions are unusual."

Two hours later, the same captain wrote: "Due to the strong winds and lack of fish, we are turning back. Our boat has struck something and I am calling the Coastguard for help."

At 9.56 pm, the captain of the *Bingo-Maru* had written: "The Coastguard says the *Eiko-Maru* is in serious trouble. We are 120 kilometres away, and the storm has now reached us. We keep hearing strange noises...."

By 10.23 pm, the crew of the *Bingo-Maru* had found the wreck of the other boat: "We can see the remains of the *Eiko-Maru*, but no survivors. The storm is very strong, and there are loud noises. We can see something moving under the water!"

When the logbooks were found washed up on Odo Island the next day, the Coastguard, who kept watch over the waters around the island, ordered a search to be carried out. But the boats and their men were nowhere to be found.

Soon, there were reports of other strange disappearances in the local newspapers. Rumours of a dangerous creature began to spread.

The Prime Minister of Japan sent the Navy to search the spot where the boats had vanished. The Navy's ships dropped bombs, hoping to destroy anything that lived at the bottom of the ocean.

Beneath the water, a giant creature stirred. Slowly, it rose to the surface. It was huge and green, with long, sharp claws and angry eyes. It wanted revenge for being attacked. The creature swiped at the ships with its claws, crushing some of them beneath its enormous feet.

The Prime Minister sent Army tanks to shoot at the creature. This made the beast even more mad. It climbed out of the water and started breathing fire, aiming a long beam of flames at the tanks.

After destroying the tanks, the fire-breathing monster stormed into the nearest city. People screamed and fled. The furious creature set buildings on fire and ripped trains from their tracks.

The Prime Minister began to panic. Nothing seemed to stop this beast! He asked for help from every scientist in the land. They needed to find out what this mysterious creature was. Perhaps if they knew, they could calm it down, or, if that didn't work, destroy it for good.

A scientist called Doctor Serizawa thought he knew where the monster had come from. He knew that the government had been testing bombs in the waters around Odo Island – at the same place where the fishing boats had disappeared.

Doctor Serizawa decided that the tests must have woken the beast, bringing it from the bottom of the ocean to the surface. He named the beast 'Godzilla'.

Doctor Serizawa had a weapon called an 'Oxygen Destroyer'. It was so powerful that it could strike down any living thing. The Prime Minister asked Doctor Serizawa if they could use this weapon to destroy Godzilla. The doctor agreed.

The next day, a large group of Navy ships travelled out into the ocean. They aimed the powerful Oxygen Destroyer at Godzilla and fired. Within minutes, Godzilla had slipped back into the ocean, and vanished.

Today, many people say that Godzilla survived and still lurks at the bottom of the dark ocean. Has the beast gone for good? Or might Godzilla return one day...?

The End

CREATING THE CREATURE

First appearances

Godzilla was first seen in the movie *Gojira*, in 1954. The film was also called *Japan under the Terror of the Monster*. Its creator, Ishiro Honda, went on to direct a number of movies about the monster, including *King Kong vs. Godzilla* and *All Monsters Attack*. Over 28 movies have now been made about the beast, and its name is known all over the world.

The name 'Gojira' (Godzilla) comes from the words 'Gorira', which means 'gorilla', and 'Kujira', which means 'whale'. This huge creature was described as a type of dinosaur with rough skin, a long tail and leaf-shaped spines that would light up when it breathed out its deadly fire.

Godzilla in comics

Godzilla has featured in many comic books in Japan and the United States. Marvel Comics made a whole series called *Godzilla, King of the Monsters*.

Godzilla on TV

The creature had its own animation series between 1978 and 1981, called *The Godzilla Power Hour*. In this series, Godzilla protected some scientists who were threatened by other monsters.

Godzilla's power and skills

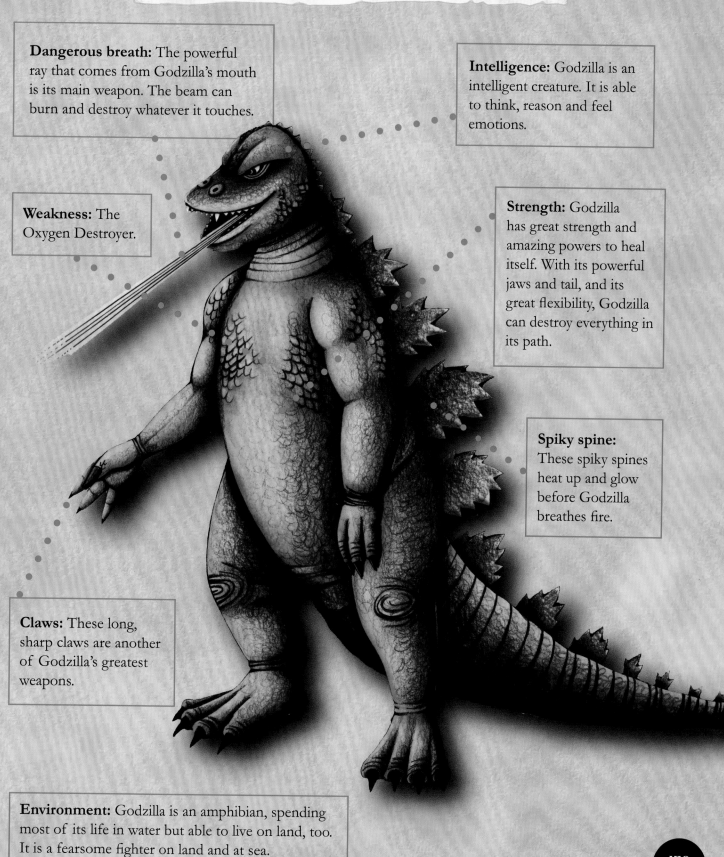

Dangerous breath: The powerful ray that comes from Godzilla's mouth is its main weapon. The beam can burn and destroy whatever it touches.

Intelligence: Godzilla is an intelligent creature. It is able to think, reason and feel emotions.

Weakness: The Oxygen Destroyer.

Strength: Godzilla has great strength and amazing powers to heal itself. With its powerful jaws and tail, and its great flexibility, Godzilla can destroy everything in its path.

Spiky spine: These spiky spines heat up and glow before Godzilla breathes fire.

Claws: These long, sharp claws are another of Godzilla's greatest weapons.

Environment: Godzilla is an amphibian, spending most of its life in water but able to live on land, too. It is a fearsome fighter on land and at sea.

THE MONSTROUS FACTS

Pteranodon

Prehistoric creatures

About 215 million years ago, dinosaurs ruled the Earth and pterosaurs ruled the skies. Huge reptiles swam in the oceans. This was the beginning of the Mesozoic Era, also known as the Age of Reptiles.

Dinosaurs

The word 'dinosaur' comes from two Greek words meaning 'terrible lizard'. Some dinosaurs were as tall as a six-storey building, while others were no larger than a chicken. Scientists have divided dinosaurs into different groups.

Theropods: These were mostly meat-eating dinosaurs, and moved on two legs. Two main examples are the *Tyrannosaurus rex* and *Velociraptor*.

Sauropods: These were plant-eaters with very long tails and necks. One of the largest dinosaurs in this group is the *Apatosaurus*.

Ankylosaurs: These plant-eating dinosaurs had thick legs and protective armour on their bodies. Some, such as the *Ankylosaurus*, had a big piece of bone in their tail for defence.

Stegosaurs: These four-legged, plant-eating dinosaurs also had protective armour. Some had spines on their body or tail. Examples include the *Kentrosaurus* and the *Stegosaurus*.

Ornithopods: These plant-eating dinosaurs used their two back legs to run. Some had colourful head crests, and a snout like a duck's bill. Examples include the *Iguanodon* and the *Parasaurolophus*.

Tyrannosaurus rex

Apatosaurus

Ceratopsians: These plant-eating dinosaurs moved on four legs. Most, such as the *Triceratops*, had one or more horns.

Pachycephalosaurs: These plant-eating dinosaurs walked on two legs. They had large, heavy skulls that they used for fighting. Examples include the *Pachycephalosaurus* and the *Stegoceras*.

Pterosaurs

Pterosaur means 'winged reptile'. These flying reptiles were seen in the skies during the Mesozoic Era. Some were as small as a pigeon while others (such as *Quetzalcoatlus*) measured up to 15 metres when their wings were spread wide. Pterosaurs were not dinosaurs themselves, and their close relatives included the *Pteranodon* and the *Rhamphorynchus*.

Water-based reptiles

A number of different reptiles adapted to life in water. These included the ichthyosaurs (with bodies similar to dolphins), plesiosaurs (some with long necks, rounded bodies and paddle-shaped legs) and mosasaurs (with long fins and lots of teeth). There were also giant sea turtles, such as *Archelo*, and crocodiles living in rivers and lakes, as they do today.

Extinction!

About 65 million years ago, most dinosaurs disappeared forever and became extinct. We do not know the exact cause of this, but many scientists think a change in the climate was to blame. Others think a huge space rock, or asteroid, may have hit Earth.

Whatever the cause, this extinction meant that a group of mammals began to change in order to survive on Earth. Scientists have recently shown that some dinosaurs escaped the extinction. One type, for example, evolved into the birds we see today.

Stegosaurus

Triceratops

Stegoceras

Ankylosaurus

Parasaurolophus

155

THE LABORATORY

A watery experiment

What do you need?
- A container
- Water
- A plastic bag
- A large rubber band

1 Half fill the container with water.

2 Put your hand into the plastic bag. Carefully stretch the rubber band over the bag and put it around your wrist, to hold the bag in place. Make sure the rubber band isn't too tight.

3 Slowly lower your hand into the water.

What happened?
The bag stuck to your hand! When you put your hand in the water, the plastic bag was pushed against your hand by the weight of the water. This shows that water is not weightless.

ZOMBIES

A SPOOKY STORY

Andrea Romero woke up and turned on the television. The screen was blank. She flicked through the channels but they were all the same. "That's odd," thought Andrea, and she got out of bed.

Suddenly, she heard the sound of glass shattering downstairs. Someone was breaking into her house!

Andrea went quietly down the stairs and came face to face with a very strange-looking man. He had cuts all over his body, and was making a terrible groaning noise. Andrea was a nurse and had seen similar wounds at the hospital, but she had never seen anyone looking this bad!

Realizing she was in danger, Andrea grabbed her car keys and bag, and ran out the front door. She jumped into her car, and drove off. The monster-like man tried to chase after her, but thankfully, he couldn't keep up.

Driving along, Angela noticed that the streets were deserted. Everything around her had been destroyed. Doors hung from their hinges, windows were smashed and empty cars sat on the pavement.

In the distance, Andrea saw hundreds of people. As she drove closer, she realized something was wrong. The people were all shuffling along, groaning. They looked just like the man who had broken into her house. Andrea realized that these weren't people – they were zombies! But where had they all come from?

Andrea decided that the hospital would be the best place to go. Surely someone there would know what had happened? She turned her car around, and sped away from the zombies.

As she drove, Andrea thought about her friends and family. She thought about calling them on her mobile phone, but before she could pull over, a zombie crossed the road out of nowhere! Andrea swerved and crashed into a big tree. She wasn't hurt, but the car was badly damaged.

In her rear-view mirror, Andrea saw a zombie coming towards her. She opened the car door and ran as fast as she could towards the woods nearby.

As Andrea ran, she heard gunshots. She looked behind her. The zombie had been shot!

Andrea ran into the woods and saw a man with a gun standing with some women and children. They all looked normal. They weren't zombies!

Andrea rushed towards them and they all hugged each other. As Andrea followed her new friends further into the woods, they told her that the city was filled with zombies, and that all of the phone lines were down.

Andrea had been lucky to escape – if the zombie had bitten her, she would have become a zombie herself!

The group walked deeper into the woods, towards an old summer house. They stayed there, taking turns to guard the house and shooting any zombies that came their way.

After a couple of days, the group began to run out of food. They needed a plan. They had to leave the safety of the summer house, but where could they go?

To plan their escape, they decided to watch the zombies and find out more about them....

Andrea and another woman soon discovered that the zombies would not cross the nearby river. They realized the zombies could not swim. They must be frightened of water! The only safe place to live would be on an island, surrounded by water.

The group gathered their belongings and loaded up a couple of trucks. They planned to drive to a dock at the edge of the woods, where they could find a boat to carry them across the water to a nearby island.

Their trip was peaceful at first. But, as the trucks got closer to the dock, zombies began to attack. Some of the men got out of the trucks, shooting at the zombies. Meanwhile, Andrea and the others ran towards a boat.

Luckily, the boat was empty. Not a zombie in sight! When everyone in the group had safely climbed aboard, they sailed off towards the island. Their plan had worked!

The group built their own little town on the island, and lived there happily. At last, they were safe. They never saw another zombie again!

THE END

CREATING THE CREATURE

What is a Zombie?

Modelo Francés - Salterio de Robert de Lisle

In science fiction, zombies are people who have been brought back from the dead. They are also known as the 'living dead'.

Some people in Haiti, in the Caribbean, worship a god called Damballa, who protects them from zombies. These people also believe that, to become a zombie, you have to drink a special potion, stay unburied and then be brought back to life by a wizard!

Zombie Stories

Stories about zombies were first told towards the end of the 17th century. Since then, zombies have featured in many myths and legends, alongside other creatures, such as mummies.

In 1697, the Frenchman Paul-Alexis Blessebois wrote a play called *Great Peru's Zombie*, about the living dead. Then, in 1789, another Frenchman, Moreau de Saint-Mery, wrote about the Caribbean island of Santo Domingo, mentioning zombies in his work.

Moreau de Saint-Mery

Edgar Allan Poe featured zombies in his stories *The Fall of the House of Usher* and *The Facts in the Case of M. Valdemar*. He inspired the author H. P. Lovecraft to write about the living dead in one of his stories, *The Case of Charles Dexter Ward*.

The explorer and journalist William Seabrook also described zombie-like creatures in his book *The Magic Island*, published in 1929.

More recently, an Italian author called Carlos Sisí wrote about zombies taking over the world in his book, *The Walkers*.

American author, H. P. Lovecraft

Meanwhile, Richard Matheson's book, *I Am Legend*, tells the story of the last living man in Los Angeles. Everyone else turns into zombies when a terrible illness breaks out. In 2007, this story was made into a movie, starring Will Smith as the main character.

George Andrew Romero

George Andrew Romero is a movie director, writer and actor, known for making zombie horror movies. Romero was born in New York City on 4 February 1940. As a child, he enjoyed making black-and-white home movies using a small camera. He started his career filming short movies and commercials. Today, Romero is known as the creator of the very first zombie movies.

Night of the Living Dead was first shown in 1968. This black-and-white movie for adults showed violent man-eating zombies. In 2001, the movie was named one of the 100 best thrillers of all time. *Time* magazine named it the 25th best horror movie in history.

After making some other movies, Romero released *Dawn of the Dead* in 1978 and *Day of the Dead* in 1985. By 2010, three more movies had been made: *Land of the Dead* (2005), *Diary of the Dead* (2007) and *Survival of the Dead* (2009). All of them featured zombies!

STRANGE BUT TRUE

People think that zombies were once normal people who caught the Zombie virus and began to look for other humans to infect as well.

According to the stories, zombies are slow and awkward because they don't get enough oxygen to breathe properly — but they are still very dangerous when they hunt in packs!

The word 'zombie' first came into general use in 1929, when the writer William B. Seabrook published a book called The Magic Island, which described a real-life encounter with 'the walking dead' while travelling in Haiti.

It is very hard to kill a zombie, mainly because they are already dead! It is said that the best way to destroy them is to do extensive damage to their brain, either by shooting them or bashing them in the head with a heavy object — ouch!

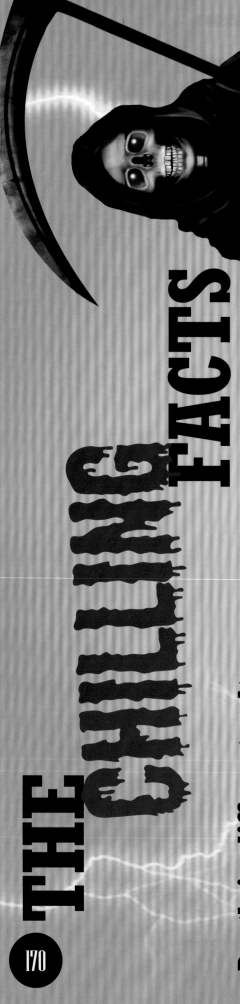

THE CHILLING FACTS

Death in different cultures

All living creatures have to die at some point, including human beings. People are often afraid of dying, and wonder if there is any kind of life after death. All around the world, people have tried to answer this question, with their own ideas about death, and what happens afterwards.

Death as a person

In Greek legends, death was shown as a character called the 'Grim Reaper', or the 'Angel of Death'. Later, in the 15th century, death was shown in drawings and paintings as a skeleton figure carrying a cutting tool called a scythe. This scary figure was sometimes dressed in a long black robe. In some examples, the 'Grim Reaper' caused the death of a victim.

The ancient Egyptians

Life after death was very important to the ancient Egyptians. They believed that the human spirit continued to live after death, as long as the body remained in one piece. They stopped a body from rotting by turning it into a mummy. They carefully washed the dead body, removed most of its organs and let it dry out. Then they covered the body in oil before wrapping it in cloth and burying it.

The Greeks and Romans

The ancient Greeks and Romans believed that when someone died, their soul would travel to an underground kingdom called Hades. If a spirit wanted to rest in peace, it had to cross a river with the help of a sailor called Charon. The spirit would need a silver coin to pay for Charon's help. That is why many Greek and Roman skeletons have since been found with a single silver coin in their grave.

Day of the Dead

In Mexico, the 'Day of the Dead' is a celebration to remember those who have died. Different symbols are used in the celebration, such as skeletons and colourful skulls.

Another life

Some people believe in reincarnation. They say that, after death, a person's spirit or soul is born again, into a new body. This idea has been around for hundreds of years. It is followed in many religions, such as Hinduism, Buddhism and Taoism.

Heaven and hell

Members of other religions, such as Judaism, Islam and Christianity, talk about life after death. They believe that when someone dies, they are judged by the way they have lived their life. They say that if a person has been good, they will go to heaven – a place where they will be happy forever. But if they have done bad things, they might go to hell – a place of suffering.

Make a moving skeleton

What do you need?
- A piece of paper
- A pair of scissors
- Glue
- Craft paper, cardboard or foam
- A hole punch
- String, elastic or split pins

Be careful when using scissors!

1 Draw a picture of a skeleton on the piece of paper, or photocopy the picture opposite.

2 Stick your picture onto craft paper, cardboard or foam.

3 Cut out the different parts of the skeleton. Use the picture opposite as a guide for which parts to cut out.

4 Use the hole punch to make holes in the shoulders, elbows, hips and knees of your model skeleton. Again, use the picture opposite to help you.

5 Use string, elastic or split pins to tie the bones together. Now the limbs of your skeleton can move!

173

BIGFÖÖT
A CREEPY STORY

For a long time, some friends and I had been planning a weekend in the mountains. Finally, we packed our tents, blankets and food, and set off. We also took our cameras, hoping to get some photos of the beautiful Crystal Mountain.

We arrived safely and began walking on foot. Soon, we met a group of cheerful mountain climbers, and decided to join them.

There was a shy young man in the group, called Aaron. As we walked, Aaron told me a sad story. Ten years ago, Aaron's parents had disappeared on Crystal Mountain, never to be seen again. Around the time of their disappearance, there had been rumours of a large, ape-like creature on the mountain. But Aaron did not know if the rumours were true. Every year, he returned to the spot where his parents were last seen, to remember them.

We continued on our way, pausing to take photographs every now and then. A few hours later, we reached base camp, where we stopped to rest.

We put up our tent and lit a fire, but, as we began to cook our dinner, we heard voices shouting. Some men came racing down the mountain towards us. Two of their group had gone missing!

Before long, we had gathered a search party, and twelve of us set off up the mountain.

After several hours, we found two torn backpacks. Next to the backpacks, we saw giant footprints in the snow. I looked at Aaron. Could these footprints belong to the same creature that had killed his parents? Aaron was very quiet. He had just seen a large, hairy beast disappear into the trees....

Suddenly, a thick fog crept in. Realizing we were not skilled mountain climbers, my friends and I decided to go back to base camp. The others, including Aaron, carried on up the mountain, looking for the missing men.

When my friends and I got back to base camp, we climbed inside our tents and zipped them up to keep warm. The fog was getting thicker and it was beginning to snow.

The rest of the search party was soon lost in the fog. With no tents, they huddled together in the snow. Aaron decided to write about the day's events in his journal. "The giant ape must be real," he wrote. "And it must still be out there...."

As the night went on, the weather got worse, and the temperature dropped sharply. With no tents or fire to warm them, Aaron and all but one of the search party froze to death.

After a difficult night, that man bravely climbed down the mountain to find us at base camp, and explained what had happened. Then he pulled Aaron's journal from his jacket, and read the last page aloud. It described the huge ape-like creature living in the mountains. The men must have spotted him before they died!

We didn't wait for the survivor to finish reading. In a hurry, we packed up our belongings and raced back down the mountain. When we finally got home, we all spent a few days recovering, glad to be safe from the monster we named 'Bigfoot'.

THE END

CREATING THE CREATURE

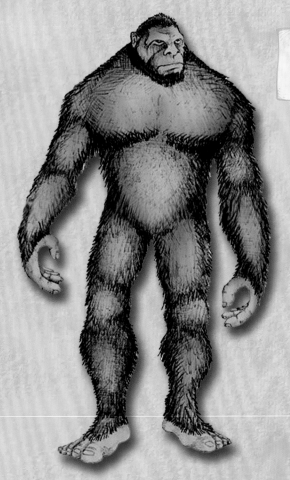

Who is the Monster?

Bigfoot is also known as 'Sasquatch', which means 'wild man'. He looks like a large ape and is thought to live in the wild forests of North America. People have reported seeing similar creatures in other countries, too. In Tibet, that creature is known as the 'Yeti'; in Australia, he is called 'Yowie'; and in South America, he is named 'Mapinguari'.

Whatever the name, the description of this creature remains the same: he is about 2 metres tall, and he is covered with brown tangled hair. Compared with the rest of his body, his head looks small.

Most people think Bigfoot isn't real. They say people have imagined him. But others believe he is a relative of the *Gigantopithecus*, a type of ape that lived about one million years ago.

Scientists think the *Gigantopithecus* were the largest apes that ever lived. They were nearly 3 metres tall, and weighed up to 550 kilograms. That's three times the size of a gorilla! Some scientists think it is possible that a descendant of the *Gigantopithecus* could still survive today.

Photo of Rene Dahinden with the statue of Bigfoot

Gigantopithecus

Does Bigfoot Exist?

The first report of Bigfoot was printed in a newspaper in 1851. In this story, two hunters saw an unknown beast among a flock of sheep. When the beast saw the hunters, it ran away.

A man called Albert Ostman said he was kidnapped by Bigfoot in 1924, while out camping. He claimed that one night, the beast took him in his sleeping bag and carried him through the woods for about three hours. Ostman said that, at dawn, he saw four Bigfoot beasts, before finally managing to escape.

In 1967, Roger Patterson and Bob Gimlin claimed to catch Bigfoot on camera in North California. They filmed what seemed to be a giant ape-like creature, covered in fur. It moved through the trees, then disappeared into the forest.

Albert Ostman speaking to author John Green

Although these sightings are rare, many people travel to the United States in search of Bigfoot. Many hunters say they have seen the beast and insist that Bigfoot is real. There are even festivals to celebrate the creature!

People who claim to have seen Bigfoot say the creature makes a kind of whooping, whistling sound. Bigfoot is thought to eat mainly a vegetarian diet, only occasionally eating meat. He is thought to live alone, sleeping during the day and leaving his shelter at night. Believers in Bigfoot say that the main evidence, of course, are the large footprints that give Bigfoot his name!

Robert Michael Pyle
Robert was born in 1947 in Denver. He has published many books, articles and poems, one of which is about Bigfoot. While trekking across the Cascade Mountains in Washington, Pyle claimed to see footprints measuring 40 centimetres long and over 20 centimetres wide.

René Dahinden
René was a famous Zoologist who researched Bigfoot. He wrote the book Sasquatch, which was published in 1973.

STRANGE BUT TRUE

Eyewitnesses describe Bigfoot as a large ape-like creature, ranging between 2–3 metres tall, and covered in dark brown or dark red hair. Some say he also has a strong, unpleasant smell!

Bigfoot is also known as the 'sasquatch', a word taken from the Halkomelem language used by one of the native tribes of north-western America, where the creature has most often been seen.

Experts estimate that an adult Bigfoot weighs around 400 kilograms. That's more than the combined weight of two of the largest living gorillas on Earth today!

The Siskiyou National Forest in the southern part of Jackson County, Oregon, is home to the world's only Bigfoot trap! It was built in 1974 and operated for six years, but during that time it caught only bears.

THE BEASTLY FACTS

Real, until proven fake

Scientists find new animal species all the time, especially in tropical jungles and oceans. Even today, there are parts of the world that haven't been fully explored. In many cases, we are still looking for proof as to whether or not a certain species exists.

Some scientists think monsters such as Bigfoot exist only in stories, and that people who report sightings are mistaken, or have been tricked. Other scientists work to find proof that monsters such as Bigfoot are real. Here are a few other strange creatures that may or may not exist....

Jersey Devil

According to legend, this strange creature first appeared in the forests of New Jersey, United States. Witnesses say the Devil is the size of a human, standing at about 1.8 metres tall. They say it has horns and wings, and the legs of a horse. They also say it is covered in fur.

The Jersey Devil has been blamed for the disappearance of people in New Jersey. Legends say that the creature is the son of a witch, but others believe it is an unknown kind of mammal.

During the 19th century, Joseph Bonaparte (older brother of the French general, Napoleon Bonaparte) saw the beast in a field in Pine Barrens, the place where some people believe it lives. Many people alive today also claim to have seen this fearsome creature.

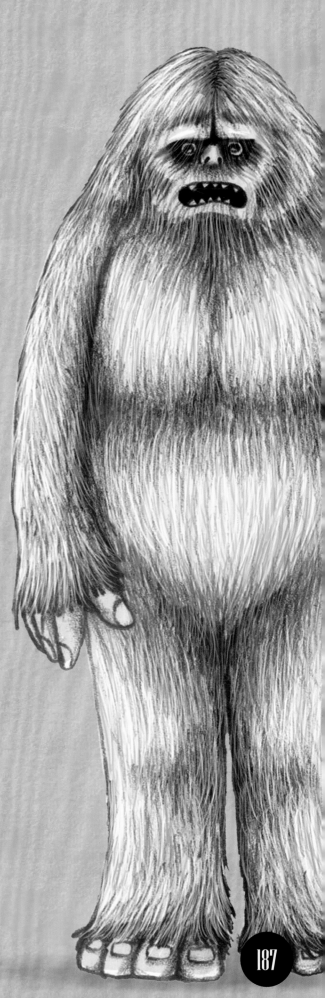

Lightning Bird
The Lightning Bird is a mythological creature in the folklore of the tribes of South Africa. It takes the form of a black and white bird, the size of a human, which is said to summon thunder and lightning with its wings and talons.

Yeti
The Yeti is also known as the 'Abominable Snowman'. This giant ape is said to live in the woods of the Himalayan mountains, north of India. People say it is a relative of the orangutan, and a descendant of *Ramapithecus*, an ape-like creature that lived in the mountains millions of years ago.

Descriptions of the Yeti suggest it is a relative of Bigfoot, and of another mythical beast called the Wendigo. Buddhist monks in the Himalayas keep ornaments of the Yeti in their monasteries. However, scientists think it would be difficult for a giant ape to survive in the cold mountains.

Marine monsters
Other unknown species are reported to live in the world's waters. Some examples include: Ogopogo (in Lake Okanagan, Canada); Mokele-Mbembe (in Lake Mamfe, Cameroon); and Nahuelito (in Lake Nahuel Huapi, Argentina). All of these stories are similar, describing a giant reptile with a long neck, like Nessie.

For hundreds of years, there have also been tales of large monsters living in the oceans. The main ones are the Kraken (a gigantic squid-like creature) and giant sea snakes.

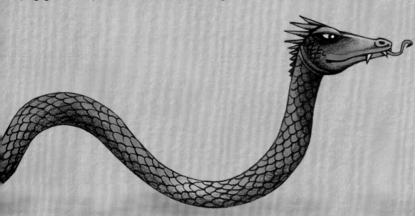

THE LABORATORY

A mysterious cloud

Gigantopithecus

What do you need?
- An empty, see-through plastic bottle with a lid
- Water
- A sheet of black paper
- A table

1 Pour some water into the bottle. Now empty the bottle.

2 Put the lid on the bottle and wrap your arms around it, squeezing tightly. Hold the bottle for a while to make it warn

3 Put the black paper on the table.

4 Lie the bottle on its side, on top of the paper. You should be able to see the black paper through the bottle.

5 Remove the lid and gently squeeze the bottle. Watch carefully. What do you see coming out of the bottle?

What happened?
A cloud came out of the bottle! When you squeezed the bottle, the air was pushed together. This warmed the drops of water left in the bottle, and turned them into a gas (or water vapour).

When you removed the lid, a bit of this water vapour came out and appeared as a little cloud!

Make Bigfoot appear!

What do you need?
- A small square of white paper, measuring about 2.5 centimetres across
- Coloured pencils
- Sticky tape
- An empty cake tin or bowl that you can't see through
- A table
- A jug of water
- A friend or family member to surprise

Draw a small picture of Bigfoot on the piece of paper. Tape your picture inside the cake tin, in the middle of the base.

Place the cake tin on top of a table in a well-lit room.

Ask your friend to keep an eye on Bigfoot as he or she slowly backs away from the tin. Tell your friend to stop as soon as the tin just blocks Bigfoot from view.

Ask your friend to stand still while you slowly pour water into the cake tin. What does your friend see?

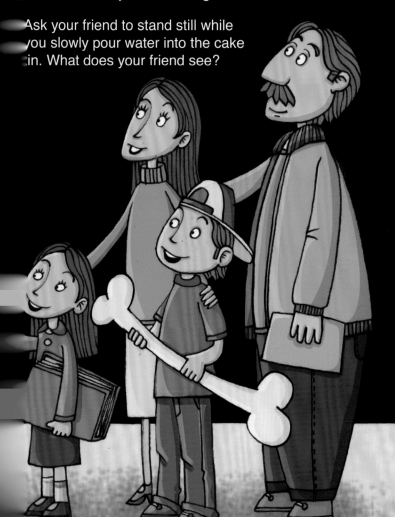

What happened?
When you poured enough water into the cake tin, your friend saw Bigfoot reappear! As water filled the tin, the reflection of the drawing bent around the tin to the surface of the water, making your friend think that Bigfoot reappeared.

The Strange Case of
DR JEKYLL
and MR HYDE

Original story by
Robert Louis Stevenson

Gabriel Utterson and Inspector Newcomen broke down the door to Dr Henry Jekyll's room. Gabriel hadn't seen his friend for days, and was beginning to worry about him. Meanwhile, the inspector wanted to see Henry in connection with a very mysterious case.

When they walked in, the two men found a dead body on the floor. It was the body of a hideous monster, but it wore Dr Jekyll's clothes! Inspector Newcomen found a piece of paper next to the monster. It was a letter for Utterson. It read:

"My dear friend, Gabriel. If you are reading this letter, it means that I, or better still, we, are now dead. I will try to explain everything that has happened....

As you know, I have always believed that there is a battle between the good and bad inside every person. This battle causes the person to suffer. There appeared to be no cure for this, but I have worked hard to find the answer.

After many experiments, I discovered a special potion that separates the good and bad parts of human nature. Feeling curious, I tested the potion on myself.

I soon realized that the separation of my good and bad sides came with a price. Every time I drank the potion, it changed me into a dreadful monster. This evil creature was unable to do anything good. Its name was Mr Hyde.

At first, I didn't mind changing into Mr Hyde. All my bad thoughts could be set free. I felt that the real me, Henry Jekyll, couldn't be blamed for Mr Hyde's actions. I drank a different potion to return to my normal self, and I thought I had Mr Hyde under control. But I was wrong.

You'll have heard rumours of a monster doing terrible things all over the city.... This monster was Mr Hyde. It was part of me!

At first, I only changed into Mr Hyde after drinking the potion. But then I began to change into him without the potion. Hyde was free to do all the wicked things he wanted to do. He was taking over!

Do you remember the mysterious death of Dr Lanyon? Lanyon saw Mr Hyde take the potion that turned him back into me, Henry Jekyll. This shocked Lanyon so much that he went mad and ended his own life. I felt terrible!

Just when I thought things couldn't get any worse, Mr Hyde murdered a gentleman called Sir Danvers Carew. Hyde had no reason to kill him. And he seemed to enjoy it! I was horrified.

After Sir Danvers' murder, the police began to look for me. I locked myself in my room and quickly drank the potion to turn back into Jekyll. I hoped that Mr Hyde would go away....

But as the days went by, things got worse. The changes happened more often, and I needed larger amounts of the potion to return to my normal self.

An important ingredient of the potion has now run out.
If I become Mr Hyde again, I will have no way of changing
back into Dr Henry Jekyll.

As I write this letter, I can feel Mr Hyde trying to take over.
It will be the last time. Will Mr Hyde be punished for his
crimes? Or will he choose to take his own life? Whatever
happens, I know this is the end of me!"

Gabriel Utterson finished reading the letter. He was shocked
and extremely sad. He looked at the monster lying on the floor
and knew that it was Mr Hyde. Hyde had killed himself, and
Henry Jekyll had died with him.

So, that was how the life of Gabriel's friend had ended. The
strange and sad case of Dr Jekyll and Mr Hyde was solved!

The End

CREATING THE CREATURE

Robert Louis Stevenson

Robert Louis Stevenson

Robert Louis Stevenson is best known for his novels and poems. Some of his most famous works include *Treasure Island, Kidnapped* and *The Strange Case of Dr Jekyll and Mr Hyde*. Stevenson's story about Jekyll and Hyde explores the idea that a person can have different personalities and ways of behaving. His story still inspires authors and movie makers today.

Robert was born in Edinburgh, Scotland, on 13 November 1850. He was the only son of Thomas and Margaret Isabella Stevenson. Robert was ill for most of his childhood and, to pass the time, his nanny told him gruesome stories that both frightened and fascinated him. Robert's mother kept a diary about her son's life, recording his childhood. She noted that Robert liked to write stories.

In 1880, Robert Stevenson married Fanny Osbourne. Eight years later, the couple went on a journey to the Samoa Islands, in the South Pacific. They lived there for several years. The islanders called him 'Tusitala', which means 'Teller of Tales'. His poor health eventually got the better of him, and Robert Louis Stevenson died on 3 December 1894, at the age of 44.

Stevenson and family on the Samoa Islands

The Strange Case of Dr Jekyll and Mr Hyde

In 1885, Robert Louis Stevenson had a nightmare that inspired him to write the story of Dr Jekyll and Mr Hyde.

He wrote the tale in just three days!

In the beginning, his work was sold to a small publisher. But in January 1886, *The Times* newspaper wrote a very good review about the book. It was soon popular around the world. *The Strange Case of Dr Jekyll and Mr Hyde* became one of the most famous detective stories of all time.

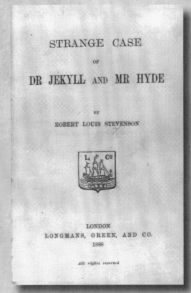

First edition of the work in 1886

Illustrations for the 1904 edition of the story

STRANGE BUT TRUE

The Strange Case of Dr Jekyll and Mr Hyde was first published as a cheap shocker in January 1886, selling close to 40,000 copies over six months. Even Queen Victoria herself may have bought a copy!

At the time the novel was written, some people believed that the way a person looked affected their ability to commit a crime. This may be why Robert Louis Stevenson showed Mr Hyde as being so ugly, deformed and hairy.

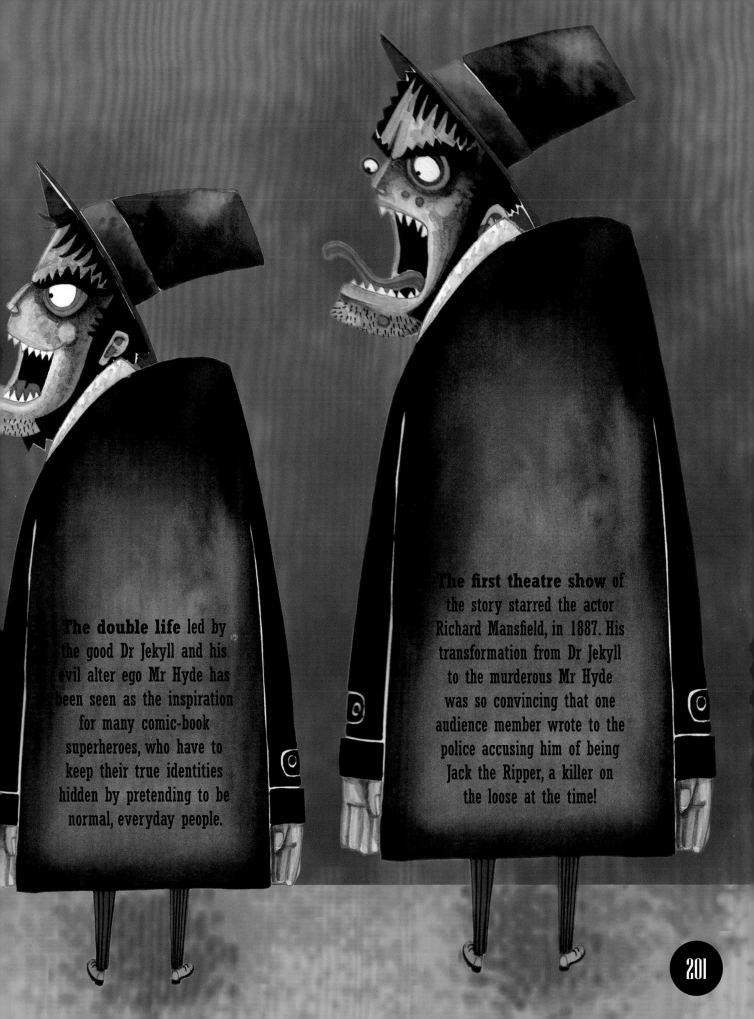

The double life led by the good Dr Jekyll and his evil alter ego Mr Hyde has been seen as the inspiration for many comic-book superheroes, who have to keep their true identities hidden by pretending to be normal, everyday people.

The first theatre show of the story starred the actor Richard Mansfield, in 1887. His transformation from Dr Jekyll to the murderous Mr Hyde was so convincing that one audience member wrote to the police accusing him of being Jack the Ripper, a killer on the loose at the time!

THE LABORATORY

The magic balloon potion

What do you need?
- A small bottle with a thin neck
- Vinegar
- Water
- A funnel or drinking straw
- Baking soda
- A balloon

Adult supervision required.
Warning! Children under eight years can choke or suffocate on uninflated or broken balloons. Keep uninflated balloons from children. Discard broken balloons at once.

1. Carefully pour a small amount of vinegar into the bottle, until there is about a centimetre in the bottom.

2. Now pour a small amount of water into the bottle, until the mixture of vinegar and water is about 2 centimetres from the bottom.

3. Carefully stretch the open part of the balloon around the tube of the funnel. Pour baking soda through the funnel, into the balloon, until the balloon is about half full.

   If you don't have a funnel, you can use a straw to fill the balloon. Stick your straw into the baking soda, then put your finger over the top of the straw. Lift the straw out of the baking soda, keeping your finger on the straw. Put it inside the neck of the balloon, then lift your finger and gently tap the straw to release the baking soda. Repeat this motion until the balloon is half full.

4. Remove the funnel from the balloon. Stretch the open part of the balloon over the top of the bottle, letting the heavy end of the balloon dangle. Try not to let any baking soda fall into the bottle. Make sure the balloon is tightly wrapped around the neck of the bottle.

5. Holding onto the balloon at the neck of the bottle, lift the heavy part of the balloon so all of the baking soda falls into the liquid at the bottom of the bottle. What do you see inside the bottle? What happens to the balloon?

What happened?
The balloon blew up! When the baking soda fell into the bottle, it mixed with the liquid. A special reaction took place between the baking soda and vinegar, producing bubbles of a gas called carbon dioxide. This gas then made the balloon inflate, or blow up.

WEREWOLF

A HAIR-RAISING STORY

One day, a handsome man named Harry Talboth walked into the antique store where I worked. Harry headed towards the collection of canes. In particular, he liked this one cane that had a silver top, shaped like a wolf. Harry decided to buy it.

After paying for the cane, Harry asked if I would like to go for a walk with him. At first, I refused. But Harry insisted and curiosity got the better of me, so I told him we could go later, after I had closed the store.

I was excited about meeting Harry, but I was also nervous. I did not know this man. I decided to ask my friend, Jenny, to join us for the walk.

Later that afternoon, Harry returned to meet me. He politely kissed my hand, and introduced himself to Jenny. I noticed he was already using his wolf-headed cane. Together, the three of us set off on our walk.

As we walked, Harry told stories of his travels around the world. Before we knew it, we had walked deep into a nearby forest. It was a misty evening, and daylight was fading fast. I saw a gypsy camp in the distance.

Jenny believed that gypsies had special powers. She persuaded us to go and have our fortunes read. Jenny and Harry ran ahead to find a fortune-teller.

Seconds later, I heard a loud shriek, and a cry of horror. Jenny was lying on the ground, bleeding. Her neck had been badly bitten. Harry lay next to her, unconscious. In despair, I realized Jenny was dying. I gently wrapped my cardigan around her, and went to help Harry.

When his dark brown eyes slowly opened, I asked Harry what had happened. He said they were attacked by a man shaped like a wolf – a werewolf! The beast had knocked Harry to the ground, before pouncing on poor Jenny.

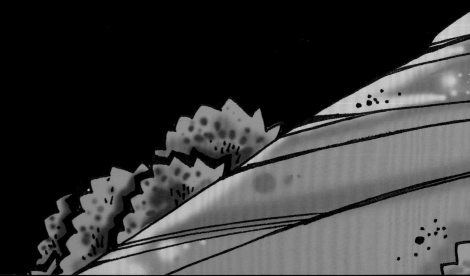

Frightened that the werewolf could still be nearby, I helped Harry to his feet. We stumbled out of the forest, towards Harry's home, Castle Talboth, where we spent a peaceful night.

The next morning, a policeman called Constable Montfort came to the store, asking questions about Jenny. I told him that a werewolf had attacked her, and that Harry and I had left her body in the forest. He told me there was no sign of Jenny anywhere in the forest. Her body had disappeared!

That night, a group of people from our village decided to search the forest for the werewolf. They set off with guns. I rushed to Harry's castle, wanting to make sure he was safe.

When I got there, I found Harry tied to a chair! He was shaking and his clothes were torn. Harry told me that Constable Montfort had tied him up, suspecting that he had killed Jenny. I agreed that was ridiculous, and untied him at once. But I noticed something wasn't quite right. Harry was much hairier than usual....

Harry and I decided to go back into the forest to look for Jenny's body. We entered the forest, a full moon shining brightly above us. As we walked towards the gypsy camp, my feet slipped on muddy ground several times. But Harry continued walking ahead.

Before I knew it, I was alone. I had lost him.

Before long, I heard a long, gruesome howl. It was the werewolf! I tried hiding behind a fat tree trunk, but it was too late. The fearsome creature had spotted me!

I shouted and struggled with the werewolf, calling for Harry. But suddenly I realized the werewolf's eyes looked familiar. It was Harry! He had turned into the werewolf! He was the one who had attacked Jenny! I closed my eyes and prayed.

Suddenly, a gun shot rang out, and the werewolf howled in pain. The search party had found us! I crawled out from beneath the werewolf's claws, and ran towards them.

"It was Harry!" I explained. "Harry was the werewolf!"

The villagers made sure the werewolf was dead, then carried me back to the village. I promised never to go out walking with a strange man ever again. Especially not one with a wolf-headed cane....

THE END

CREATING THE CREATURE

The Myth of the Werewolf

Werewolves have existed in people's imaginations for hundreds of years. They often feature in myth and legend, appearing when there is a full moon, and covered in hair from head to toe. Many books and films have been written about werewolves. But where did they come from? Who imagined the very first werewolf?

Werewolves first appeared in myths from Ancient Greece. One of these stories is over 2000 years old. It describes a fierce and cruel king, called Lycaon. This king put many people in prison, and killed them if he did not like them. He also refused to believe in the gods.

According to the story, Zeus – the king of the gods – heard about Lycaon's terrible behaviour.

Zeus wanted to find out more about his cruel ways, and decided to see for himself what Lycaon had been up to.

This engraving shows Zeus turning Lycaon into a werewolf

Another engraving showing Zeus turning Lycaon into a werewolf

A woodcut by Peter Stubbe, from 1589

Disguising himself as a traveller, Zeus went to visit Lycaon. The servants recognized that this man was actually a great god, and prayed to him, but Lycaon wasn't so sure. He decided to test the traveller by inviting him to dinner. Lycaon gave Zeus a selection of meats to eat, including human flesh!

Zeus knew it was a trick and did not eat the food. He was very angry.

Suddenly, a full moon covered the Sun, and lightning bolts destroyed Lycaon's palace. Lycaon cried out and ran for his life, but Zeus was more powerful than Lycaon realized. As a punishment for Lycaon's bad behaviour, Zeus turned him into a werewolf!

Lycaon's cries became growls, his nose became a snout, his teeth became pointed and he began to walk on all fours. He had the body of a wolf, but his eyes and mind were still human.

The Greek myth ends with Zeus sending Lycaon to live in the woods forever. Every full moon, Lycaon's appetite for human flesh returned. And the people he killed also became werewolves....

The word 'werewolf' comes from the Greek 'lycanthropus', meaning 'wolf man'.

lykos = wolf
anthropos = man

THE AWESOME FACTS

The Moon

The Moon is a satellite, which means it travels around the Earth in a circle, called an orbit. It is the fifth largest Moon in the Solar System, measuring over 3200 kilometres in diameter, or width. That's about a quarter of the Earth's diameter. It appears much smaller because it is 400,000 kilometres away! If the Earth were the size of a basketball, the Moon would be the size of a tennis ball.

Travel to the Moon

In 1959, Russia was the first country to reach the Moon with a man-made spacecraft. Soon after this, the United States sent men into space, with a mission to land on the Moon. The crew of Apollo 11 were the first people to walk on the Moon, in 1969. Their footprints are still visible on the Moon's surface because there is no wind or weather on the Moon to brush them away.

Observing the Moon

Galileo Galilei (1564–1642) was the first person to really study the Moon. Using a powerful telescope, he saw that the Moon's surface was not smooth, but covered in craters. It even had mountains and valleys, like the Earth.

Moon movements

The Moon takes just over 27 days to go all the way around the Earth. It turns while it is moving, taking about 29 days to make one full turn.

Phases of the Moon

The Moon does not make its own light. Instead, it reflects light from the Sun, appearing to glow. While the Moon is orbiting the Earth, light from the Sun reaches it from different positions. This is why the Moon appears to change shape in the sky, from one night to the next.

Week 1, New Moon: This occurs when the Moon is between the Sun and the Earth. We can't see a New Moon because the lit side is facing away from the Earth. The Moon appears dark to us, and seems to be invisible.

Week 2, First Quarter: This is when the Moon has completed one quarter of its orbit around the Earth. The right half of the Moon is lit up, appearing as a Half Moon.

Week 3, Full Moon: At this stage, the Earth is between the Sun and the Moon. Sunlight reaches the Moon on one side, so the whole face of the Moon can be seen from Earth.

Week 4, Last Quarter: The following week, the Moon has completed three quarters of its orbit around the Earth. This time, the left half of the Moon is lit up. After the fourth week, the Moon reaches its original position and disappears from view, starting the cycle again.

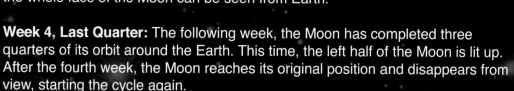

Eclipses

Occasionally the Sun, the Moon and the Earth are in a straight line.

Solar Eclipse: This happens when the Moon passes directly between the Sun and the Earth. The Moon fully or partially blocks the Sun. At least two to five solar eclipses happen each year, though a total eclipse, with the Sun fully blocked, is much more rare than a partial one.

Lunar Eclipse: This happens when the Moon passes behind the Earth, so that the Earth blocks the Sun's rays from reaching the Moon. This can only happen when the Sun, the Earth and the Moon are exactly in line, with the Earth in the middle.

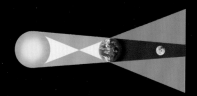

THE LABORATORY

A mini moon

What do you need?
• A hair dryer
• A table tennis ball

1. Plug in the hair dryer and turn it on. If it's not your hair dryer, ask permission from its owner first!

2. Put the hair dryer on the highest setting and point it so that cold air is blowing up, towards the ceiling.

3. Place your table tennis ball in the cold air above the hair dryer, and let go. Watch what happens.

What happened?
Your table tennis ball floated in the air! The airflow from the hair dryer pushed the ball upwards. Meanwhile, gravity was pushing down onto the ball. When the upwards and downwards forces were equal, the ball appeared to float in mid-air.

Bouncing planets

What do you need?
- A large, heavy ball, such as a basketball or football
- A smaller, light ball, such as a tennis ball or rubber ball
- An outdoor space

1 Stand outside, with plenty of space around you.

2 Keeping one hand underneath the larger ball, put the smaller ball on top of the larger ball and gently hold it there.

3 Now let go of both balls at exactly the same time. Watch what happens.

What happened?
If you dropped the balls at exactly the same time, the lighter ball should have bounced off the heavier ball, flying into the air! This is because both of the balls have energy. Energy from the heavier ball was transferred to the lighter ball when the two balls hit one another. This sent the lighter ball flying into the air.

GLOSSARY

ALIEN
A creature or being that is believed to come from another planet.

ALTER EGO
A person's 'other' personality, which is usually very different from the person's 'normal' or everyday personality.

AMAZON
The world's largest tropical rainforest and river, which is found in South America. The river flows through Peru, Colombia and Brazil into the Atlantic Ocean.

APPETITE
A strong desire for something, usually food.

ARACHNID
Any of a group of invertebrates (animals without a backbone) that has eight segmented legs, no wings or antennae and a body that is divided into two parts. One part of the body is made up of the head and thorax (the part between the head and abdomen), which are joined together. The other body part is the abdomen. Spiders, mites, scorpions and ticks are all arachnids.

ARTERY
A blood vessel that carries blood away from the heart. Arteries have muscular walls that expand and contract to help pump blood around the body.

ASTRONOMER
A scientist who studies the Universe and everything in it, including the galaxies, stars and planets.

BOLD
Describes a person who is willing to take risks and who is confident and courageous.

CANE
A thin stick that is used for walking.

CAPILLARY
A tiny blood vessel that connects the smallest arteries to the smallest veins in the body. The capillaries form a network throughout the tissues of the body. The exchange of oxygen, nutrients, waste products and carbon dioxide between the tissues and the blood all take place in the capillaries.

CARBON DIOXIDE
A gas with no colour or smell that is found in the atmosphere. Carbon dioxide is produced when animals breathe and when plant and animal materials decay. It is used by plants to produce sugars. It is also used in fire extinguishers.

CHARACTERISTIC
A feature or quality of a person, place or thing that is usually used to identify them.

CIRCULATORY SYSTEM
The system that moves blood through the body. It is made up of the heart and blood vessels.

COMMERCIAL
Describes something that makes or is intended to make money.

CRATER
A shallow, bowl-shaped hole in a surface, which is formed by an explosion or by the impact of an object.

CYLINDER
A three-dimensional shape that has straight parallel sides and a circular or oval section.

DEGREE
An academic award that is given by a college or university after a person completes a course.

DENSE
Describes a substance that is tightly packed together.

DESERTED
Describes a place that is empty of people.

DIAMETER
The length of a straight line drawn across a circle through its centre.

ECLIPSE
The partial or total blocking of light from a planet, moon or star as it passes behind or through the shadow of another planet, moon or star. In a solar eclipse the Moon comes between the Sun and the Earth. In a lunar eclipse the Moon passes through the Earth's shadow.

ELECTRIC CURRENT
A flow of electricity that is caused by the movement of electrically charged particles.

EVOLVE
To develop specific characteristics to suit the environment. For example, cats have evolved to have an excellent sense of balance.

EXTINCT
Describes plants and animals that are no longer living or that no longer exist. For example, dinosaurs and mammoths are now extinct.

FIN
One of the wing-like or paddle-like parts of a fish, dolphin or whale. The fins are used to propel, steer or balance the creature in the water.

FLYING SAUCER
A disc-shaped flying craft that is supposedly flown by aliens. A flying saucer can also be called a UFO (Unidentified Flying Object).

FORTUNE TELLER
A person who is able to predict what the future holds for another person.

FOSSIL
The hardened remains or imprints of a plant or animal that lived long ago. Fossils are often found in layers of rock and along the beds of rivers that flow through them. They have also been found in ice.

FRICTION
The resistance to movement that occurs when two objects are in contact with each other. For example, friction slows down a ball that is rolling across grass.

GILL
The organ that enables most water animals, such as fish, to take oxygen from the water. Usually, each animal has a pair of gills.

GYPSY
A member of a travelling group of people. Gypsies usually make a living by buying and selling goods.

HARNESS ELECTRICITY
To control and make use of natural resources, such as the Sun's energy or water, to make electricity in the form of solar power (from the Sun) or hydroelectric power (from water).

INVASION
The entering of a country or region by a military force to take control over it.

KIDNAP
To take someone against his or her will and hold him or her captive. Kidnappers usually ask for money before they will release their victim. This money is called a ransom.

LABORATORY
A room or building that is used for scientific experiments, research or teaching. Laboratories can also be used to produce drugs and chemicals.

LEGEND
A story that people believe to be historically accurate, but has not been proven, such as the legend of werewolves.

LOCH
Scottish name for "lake". Loch Ness is a lake where a monster is thought to live.

LOGBOOK
A regular or systematic record of the things that happen or what someone sees. A logbook is usually kept during the voyage of a ship or aircraft.

LUNAR
To do with the Moon, such as a lunar eclipse. This happens when the Moon passes behind the Earth so that the Earth blocks the Sun's rays from reaching the Moon.

MALARIA
A disease found in tropical areas and spread by female mosquitoes. Symptoms of malaria include a high fever, shaking chills, headaches, sickness and sweating. If not diagnosed and treated quickly enough, malaria can be fatal. Each year, around 1 million people die from malaria.

MARTIAN
A creature or being that comes from the planet Mars.

MEDIEVAL
Describes something to do with the Middle Ages, the period of European history from around 1000 to 1453. During the Middle Ages, separate kingdoms were formed, there was massive growth in trade and urban life, and kings and queens and the church became more powerful.

MORGUE
A place where dead bodies are taken. Morgues are sometimes also called mortuaries.

MYTH
A traditional story, especially one that is about early history or one that explains something that is naturally occurring. Myths often involve supernatural beings or events.

NATURALIST
An expert or student of natural history, which is the scientific study of animals or plants.

NAVY
The branch of a country's armed forces that conducts military operations at sea.

ORBIT
The path of a planet, moon, asteroid, comet or artificial satellite as it spins around another body. An orbit can also mean one full revolution of such a body.

ORIGAMI
The Japanese art of folding paper into shapes and figures.

PARASITE
An organism that lives in or on a different kind of living thing (called the host). Parasites usually take some or all of their nourishment from the host and are generally harmful to the host. Lice and tapeworms are parasites found on and in humans.

POLES, THE
Either of the two points at which the Earth's axis meets the Earth's surface. The Earth's poles are the North Pole and the South Pole.

RABIES
A disease of warm-blooded animals that causes swelling of the brain and spinal cord. Rabies is spread by the bite of an infected animal and in most cases it is fatal. Pets are usually vaccinated to prevent the disease.

RAY
A thin, narrow beam of heat. In the H. G. Wells' 1898 novel, *The War of the Worlds*, the Martians' main weapon is the Heat-Ray.

SATELLITE
An object that orbits a planet or asteroid. Artificial satellites are objects launched to orbit the Earth or another planet. They are used for research, communications, navigation and to help predict the weather.

SKELETON
The internal structure of vertebrates (animals with a backbone). The skeleton is made of bone or cartilage. Its main job is to support the body and protect the vital organs. There are 206 bones in the human skeleton.

SOLAR
Relating to the Sun, such as a solar eclipse. During a solar eclipse, the Moon comes between the Sun and the Earth.

SOLAR SYSTEM
The Sun together with the

eight planets (Mercury, Venus, Earth, Mars, Jupiter, Saturn, Uranus and Neptune) and all the other bodies that orbit the Sun, including moons, asteroids and comets.

SOUL
The spiritual part of a human being or other animal that is thought in some religions to live on after the person or animal has died.

SPACESHIP
A vehicle used for travelling in space that is usually controlled by a crew.

SPECIES
A group of organisms that have many characteristics in common.

SUBSTANCE
Something that you can touch or see that is usually used for making things.

TELESCOPE
A device that is used to detect and observe distant objects, such as stars or planets. Telescopes contain lenses, mirrors or both. These collect light to make an enlarged image of a distant object.

TENTACLE
A narrow, flexible part that extends from the body of certain animals, such as an octopus. These animals use their tentacles for feeling, grasping and moving.

TRANSFUSION
The transfer of blood, blood products or other fluids from one person or animal to another.

TRANSYLVANIA
A large region of north western Romania. It is separated from the rest of the country by the Carpathian Mountains and the Transylvanian Alps. The region originally belonged to Hungary but in 1918, it became part of Romania. Bram Stoker's 1897 novel *Dracula* was set in Transylvania.

UNCONSCIOUS
Describes someone who is not awake, aware of or responding to things.

UNIVERSE
Everything, including all of the planets, galaxies and everything between the galaxies, regarded as a whole.

VIGOROUS
Something that is strong, healthy and full of energy.

WITCHCRAFT
The practice of magic by witches. Witches use spells and call on the spirits, usually to do evil.

ZEPPELIN
A large, rigid German airship that was developed in the early 20th century. Zeppelins were used during World War I for bombing, and after the war to transport passengers until the 1930s.

ZOOLOGY
The branch of biology that deals with the study of animals, including their growth and structure.

FRANKENSTEIN'S MONSTER

THE LOCH NESS MONSTER

WITCHES

DRACULA

THE FLY

THE CREATURE FROM THE BLACK LAGOON

KING KONG

THE PHANTOM OF THE OPERA

THE WAR OF THE WORLDS

GODZILLA

ZOMBIES

BIGFOOT

DR JEKYLL AND MR HYDE

WEREWOLF